LOST TRA[ ]
OF
EAST ANGLIA

Leslie Oppitz

COUNTRYSIDE BOOKS
NEWBURY, BERKSHIRE

COUNTRYSIDE BOOKS
3 Catherine Road
Newbury, Berkshire

To view our complete range of books,
please visit us at
www.countrysidebooks.co.uk

ISBN 1 85306 872 1

Cover picture of a tramway inspector joining the driver
of an Ipswich tram in Cornhill, c1910,
from an original painting by Colin Doggett

Designed by Mon Mohan

Produced through MRM Associates Ltd., Reading
Typeset by Techniset Typesetters, Newton-le-Willows
Printed by Woolnough Bookbinding Ltd., Irthlingborough

CONTENTS

ACKNOWLEDGEMENTS

Acknowledgements go to the many libraries, record offices and museums throughout East Anglia where staff have delved into records. Thanks go to John H. Meredith and the late J.L. Smith of Lens of Sutton for their help in supplying many of the early pictures, and also to the following who generously contributed with information: Peggy Dowie, Chairman of the Southend Pier Foundation; Glynn Wilton of the National Tramway Museum Library, Crich; Ken Blacker of the East Anglia Transport Museum; Brian Dyes of the Ipswich Transport Museum; Mark Smith for help with old Ipswich photographs; the Bridewell Museum of Norwich; Wayne Upperton for help locating an old Wisbech & Upwell tramcar; Brian Butler for his help with a number of maps and Colin Withey for his loan of some early pictures.

Finally thanks go to my wife, Joan, for travelling East Anglia with me and also proving herself once again as an able proofreader.

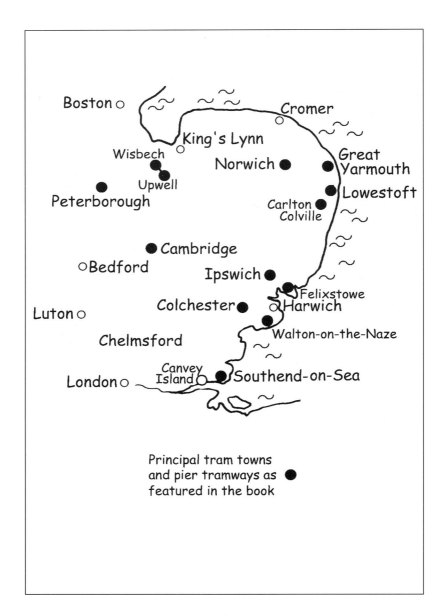

Boston ○
Cromer ○
King's Lynn ○
Wisbech ○
Upwell ●
Peterborough ●
Norwich ●
Great Yarmouth ●
Lowestoft ●
Carlton Colville ●
Cambridge ●
○ Bedford
Ipswich ●
Felixstowe
Colchester ●
Harwich ○
Luton ○
Walton-on-the-Naze ●
Chelmsford
Canvey Island ○
London ○
Southend-on-Sea ●

Principal tram towns
and pier tramways as ●
featured in the book

6

Introduction

Passengers climb aboard a double-deck electric tram and take their seats – the driver sounds his gong – and the vehicle pulls slowly away. The car seats 22 in the saloon and another 26 'on top'. A conductor punches tickets and the tram makes its way along a cobbled street, past a general store and various shops to its first stop. The scene might well have been a street in Lowestoft around the 1920s, but it happened in fact in 2003! The car was one of many superbly restored by the members of the East Anglia Transport Museum at Carlton Colville, which can be found just off the Beccles–Lowestoft (A146) road.

Trams originated in New York in 1832 and in the United States today they are still referred to as 'streetcars'. There had been great enthusiasm as two horse-drawn single-deck cars achieved 'breathtaking' speeds on the flat iron strips that served as rails. In 1860 trams reached Birkenhead, introduced to this country by an American called (inappropriately) George Francis Train. The system, just over $1\frac{1}{4}$ miles in length, opened on August 30th with the claim that it was the 'first street tramway in Europe'.

London saw its first trams in March 1861 when Train laid tracks between Marble Arch and Notting Hill Gate, with the first car pulled by two horses. Two other routes followed, one from Westminster to Victoria Station and another from Westminster Bridge to Kennington Park. George Train considered his tramcars to be transport for the wealthy although history has shown that the reverse became true.

These early systems proved popular enough but they failed in London because the wrong type of track had been chosen. A step rail was used, an L-shaped rail with a vertical section protruding above the road surface, but this became unpopular with other road users. Many horse-drawn carriages had their wheels ripped off when crossing at an angle so the lines where forced to close within a year. On the 1860 line in Birkenhead,

7

events turned out differently since the track was eventually replaced by an improved rail set flush with the road surface.

One of the early undertakings in East Anglia came about in October 1880 when a horse tramway system began services in the city of Cambridge. In 1883 steam trams began services between Wisbech and Upwell, primarily to assist agriculture in the area. Within a short time they were carrying some 3,000 passengers each week in addition to around 600 tons of goods.

When electric trams were introduced in Norwich in July 1900 they proved immediately popular and it was not long before many other towns developed their own systems. Trams came to Southend-on-Sea in July 1901 and grandiose ideas followed for tramway systems to link Southend with places such as Burnham-on-Crouch and even Colchester. But the ideas came to nothing. Such proposals generally received strong opposition from the main railway companies and there was usually insufficient financial support.

Once installed, the towns put their trams to good use. In times when most people walked because money was short, the new transport provided a cheap method of travel where previously it might not have been possible. Further electric undertakings were soon to follow. In 1902 services started at Great Yarmouth, eventually to reach Caister-on-Sea to the north and Gorleston-on-Sea to the south. During 1903 further systems opened at Lowestoft and Ipswich with many others following over the next year or so. There were plans to join the Great Yarmouth and Lowestoft systems but they came to nothing.

This book provides a comprehensive coverage of the lives of these tramways throughout the East Anglia region. It also enables readers to explore the area for themselves and view the many relics that have survived the years.

Leslie Oppitz

1

Horse Trams In A University City

Cambridge Street Tramways Company

An early picture of Cambridge single-deck car no 2 between the post office and the station, c1880s. The poor state of the road is much in evidence. (Cambridgeshire Collection)

Passers-by in the streets of Cambridge would have been surprised one day in the early 1880s to see two men pulling a tramcar carrying 57 passengers, from the railway station to the post office. The car made five stops along the route – and the men did not suffer any great strain. This was an experiment staged by the Cambridge Street Tramways Company, which had become frustrated by continual accusations that its horses

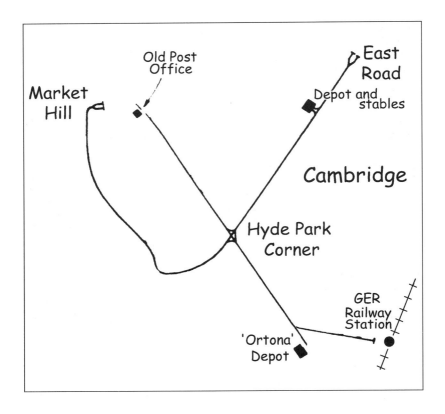

were ill-treated. Yet it was to no avail and sections of the public remained unconvinced.

In August 1851, Cambridge's first horse-buses appeared. They were double-deckers, each drawn by four horses, providing a service between Cambridge and Shepreth to connect with trains from London's Kings Cross. When the line from Shepreth was extended to Cambridge in 1852, the buses were withdrawn. In 1878 plans for horse-drawn trams were announced and two companies, each called Cambridge Tramways Company, submitted schemes. The first company proposed routes across the city centre to a gauge of 3 ft 6 ins but the other was less ambitious. It put forward ideas for a 4 ft 8½ in system from the station to the city centre plus another from Hyde Park Corner along Trumpington Street to serve the colleges.

In 1879 the Cambridge Street Tramways Company (CST) was formed and a 3 ft 6 in gauge was proposed but this changed to 4 ft before construction began. Bearing in mind the city's narrow streets, a narrower gauge was required. A Bill received Royal Assent on 21st July 1879 and work quickly went ahead. In his book, *Cambridge Street Tramways,* S.L. Swingle wrote that on 13th October 1880 a single-deck car was tried out, but there was difficulty in negotiating the section by Great St Mary's church because the gauge of the temporarily laid rails was incorrect. A further trial two days later proved successful.

The first section of the tramway opened officially on 28th October 1880 carrying passengers from the railway station along St Andrew's Street to the post office opposite Christ's College. Six cars were used and on the next day it was recorded that 801 people had travelled on the trams. The cars, comprising two double-deck open-top and four single-deck vehicles, were built by the Starbuck Car & Wagon Company. They cost £300 each and were designed for one-horse working and the livery was red and cream. There was difficulty initially in finding a suitable place to house the trams and horses and they were accommodated for a time in the goods yard at the railway station. Later, in January 1881, the depot and stables were moved to 184 East Road, where the CST's registered office was situated.

The Cambridge Street Tramways (Extension) Order of 1880 agreed further routes. In November 1880 a line from Hyde Park Corner via Lensfield Road and Trumpington Street opened to Market Hill, and later the same month trams were reaching East Road via Gonville Place. At the same time, further sections of tramway were authorised but these never materialised and the route mileage remained at 2.69 miles. Had one been completed, trams would have extended further

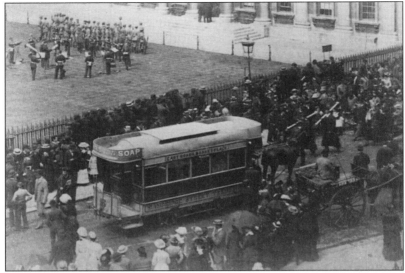

Horse tram no 5, c1890, outside the Senate House amid a University procession. Only single-deck cars were used on the Trumpington Road route. (Cambridgeshire Collection)

along East Road into Newmarket Road. This line never went beyond the junction of Fitzroy Street, just beyond the January 1881 depot. Another line, opposed by the Masters and Fellows of Emmanuel College, would have provided a circular route round part of the city. From East Road, trams would have passed along Maids' Causeway to enter Emmanuel Road and Emmanuel Street to join the existing line in St Andrew's Street.

Public complaints about the over-working of horses continued. Letters appeared in the *Cambridge Chronicle* stating that the horses were suffering because of heavy loads. It was pointed out that the need to continually stop and start a car carrying 40 or more passengers put such a strain on a single horse that two should be used per tram. The idea was tried for a time but it did not last.

Despite a fleet of only six cars, a frequent service was

maintained. Throughout the day, trams ran every ten minutes from the station to the post office and every seven minutes at busier times. Fares on any route were 2d all the way or 1d from Hyde Park Corner. Season tickets could be purchased at 6s a month or up to £2 10s for a year. Small animals or poultry could be carried at ½d per head but this was rarely put into practice.

The trams were used by many passengers to connect with trains, so it was important that time should not be lost. Yet this was not always possible, for 'up' cars to the station frequently had to wait along the route to pass 'down' cars since much of the track was single and loops had not been provided. It was not until 1885 that a passing place was constructed in Station Road. Yet the company flourished, more horses were purchased and the permanent way was improved. There were complaints that the trams were noisy and a considerable amount of money was spent to fit new wheels and noiseless springs.

There was a dispute in 1890 between the CST and the council over roadway maintenance. The 1879 Act carried a clause requiring the tramway company to repair 'the highways in which the rails were laid'. This caused much concern but the matter was resolved in 1892 when the council agreed to take over the liability, provided the tramway company paid an annual sum of £325 by quarterly instalments over a period of 25 years. Under the arrangement, the CST undertook to keep the sleepers, rails and concrete bed in good order while the council maintained the road.

During 1894 another double-deck tramcar (no 7) was purchased from Starbuck. This, like earlier double-deckers, could seat 18 in the saloon but 23 (one extra) on top. In the same year, the company's profits benefited when Cambridge held a Royal Show, with trams carrying many additional passengers during the event. In May 1895 there was a plan for trams to reach the village of Newnham from Trumpington Road by a proposed viaduct road across the meadows. According to the *Cambridge Chronicle*, this would allow 'the

Cambridge's double-deck horse tram no 7 waits at the Post Office terminus in 1904 before returning to the railway station. (Cambridgeshire Collection)

people from the slums and alleys of our congested, unhealthy towns into the green lanes and fair meadow land ...' Alas, the scheme did not succeed.

A setback to the fortunes of the CST came in 1896 when the Cambridge Omnibus Company was granted a licence to operate eight two-horse buses in the town and suburbs. This incensed the CST since the buses planned to operate a standard 1d fare from the station to the town (the trams were still 2d) and also since the CST were paying £325 a year for road repairs while the buses used the roads free of charge. The public were in favour of the buses, so the CST countered the challenge by purchasing four single-deck buses and introducing its own standard 1d fare. The buses were specially made for the CST and, because of their rather unusual design, they acquired the nickname of 'bathing machines'.

14

A comic postcard issued in Cambridge in 1905 at a time when motor buses were becoming effective competition. Similar cards were sold in other horse-tram towns. (Cambridgeshire Collection)

The CST suffered badly against the competition and in the end it was the omnibus company that offered a solution. In 1900 it agreed to withdraw its buses from tram routes if the CST withdrew its buses from the rest of the city. The CST sold its buses to its ex-competitor and tramway receipts improved. The bus company was less fortunate, lasting only until 1902 when it went out of business.

Meantime in 1898 the British Electric Traction Co Ltd purchased shares in the CST and proposed an electric tramway system. At about the same time the council applied for powers to municipalise the CST, also with a view to electrification. No agreement was reached and in 1904 the BET sold its shares to the Cambridge Electric Traction Syndicate, a subsidiary of the city's electric supply company, which was also interested in electric trams. A public meeting was held to debate the possibility but the idea was opposed because of the costs involved and objections to overhead power lines.

15

Horse trams and motor buses in competition, 1912. The Ortona Motor Co commenced services in 1907 and it was not long before they successfully operated over tramway routes. The trams lasted until February 1914. (Cambridgeshire Collection)

In 1905 ideas of electric trams were shelved when two motor bus companies commenced services. Known as the 'Cambridge Light Blue Co' and the 'Cambridge Motor Bus Co', rivalry between the concerns was strong. The 'Light Blues' lasted only six months and the second company lost its licence in September 1906. For almost a year the trams held their own but, in August 1907, the old Cambridge Motor Bus Co was bought up and relaunched as the Ortona Motor Co, with its fleet of green buses. Offices were at 112 Hills Road (later the depot of the Eastern Counties Omnibus Co), and it was not long before double-deck buses were successfully operating over tramway routes.

In 1909 a further car, a double-deck open-top, was purchased for £160 (making eight in all). Yet CST revenue

16

The remains of a Cambridge tram body photographed c1960 in a garden at Haddenham in use as a tool shed. Sadly the tram body no longer exists today. (Maurice Kidd)

continued to suffer, worsened by the £325 a year payable for road upkeep. By 1912 the CST was in arrears and in September 1913 a writ was issued against the CST for amounts outstanding. In January 1914 a petition was filed for the compulsory winding-up of the company. The motor buses had won the day – partly at the expense of the tramway company.

The end for the horse trams came on Wednesday, 18th February 1914. Local residents enjoyed last rides on the cars that had served them for 34 years and children were encouraged to travel so that they might remember the trams in the future. A mock funeral service was held by under-graduates, many wearing surplices and chanting a dirge. The official last car left the railway station at 6.25 pm driven by Ephraim Skinner, the company's oldest driver. Two days later, at an auction attended by around 600 people, sales included the cars themselves, which fetched between £7 15s and £15 each.

Today the former tram depot at East Street has been redeveloped although some of the original buildings have been converted to offices. There is another reminder of the old days at the Cambridge Museum of Technology in Cheddars Lane, where a section of tram track has been preserved and is on display. There is also a reversible type wooden seat but the slats forming the seat and back are modern replacements.

The following was part of a poem written by a driver to his horse after the closure of the tramway:

> What will I do when you are gone?
>   All day in sun and rain,
> From Station to the Post Office
>   I'll walk and back again.
> But oh! An awful thought occurs,
>   That fills me with dismay.
> They're sure to pull the tramlines up
>   And I shan't know my way.

2

Astride The Colne

Colchester Corporation Tramways

To say that Colchester, once known as Camulodunum, has a history could be considered quite an understatement. There was probably a settlement there as early as the 5th century BC and it was in AD 43 that the town was invaded by the Romans, who established a major colony. In AD 60 the Britons under Queen Boadicea massacred the Romans and destroyed the temple built by Claudius in AD 50.

It was not until Norman times, around 1085, that a castle was built on the site of the former Roman temple and in 1190 the town's charter was granted by Richard I. Today the castle keep maintains an entirely peaceful existence with, as might be expected, numerous Roman exhibits on view. There are also more recent items to be seen in the museum, among them various tramway artefacts. These include a couple of reversible seats rescued from Colchester's trams, which ceased running well over seventy years ago.

The town's tramway system lasted just 25 years with a public service commencing on 28th July 1904. The official opening was held in pouring rain, yet despite this a large crowd collected to watch the Mayoress drive the first car (no 13) from the Town Hall to Lexden, then to North Station and finally back to the Town Hall. The car, decorated with flags and bunting, carried many invited guests and led a procession of four cars.

Had an earlier company survived, Colchester might well have had a steam tramway. In 1883 Parliament approved a Provisional Order for such a system and track laying proceeded between North Station and the High Street but by

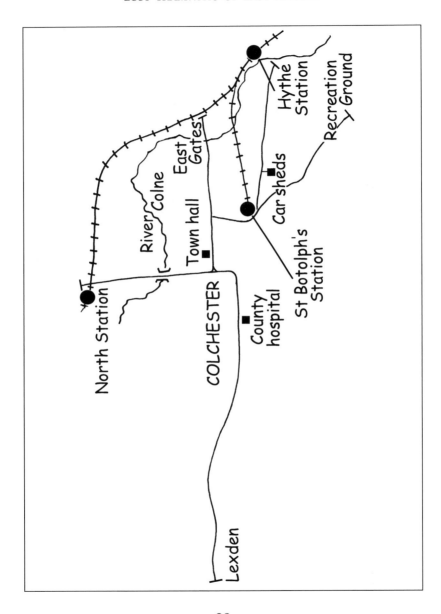

the time it reached Middleborough the company had run into financial difficulties and the plans were dropped. The track was removed and forfeited to Colchester Corporation along with all other materials.

In 1898 the British Electric Traction Company (BET) applied for a Light Railway Order to allow the introduction of electric trams on five short routes emanating from the town centre. The application was rejected by the Light Railway Commissioners on the grounds that the routes were all within the borough. The Commissioners stated that the system should be promoted as an urban tramway to be authorised under the Tramways Act of 1870. Further ideas were discussed, including an interesting scheme in 1901. The Board of Trade approved a proposal from Colchester Town Council to run 'cars or omnibuses' by overhead electric wires – but without the laying of track. Thus Colchester could have become the first town in Britain to operate trolleybuses! Subsequently Parliament agreed an Act of 1901 authorising Colchester Corporation to build and work a system using 3 ft 6 in gauge electric trams within the borough.

A number of town councillors were unsure about the decision and decided to wait and see how motor buses developed. The buses proved unreliable, although it was not until February 1903 that a vote of 18 to 9 agreed that an electric tramway should be built at an estimated cost of around £63,000. Also in 1901 there had been a proposal from a company to build a light railway from Southend to Colchester. It was expected the promoters would seek a link with the Colchester system but since the light railway proposed a gauge of 4 ft 8½ ins and the town's gauge was 3 ft 6 ins, there would have been difficulties.

The fleet initially comprised 16 cars supplied at a cost of £575 each. They were built by the Electric Railway & Tramway Carriage Works Ltd and mounted on Brill trucks. The cars were four-wheeled and open-topped with three main windows on each side. Each seated 22 passengers in the saloon where the seats were longitudinal and a further 24 'on

Car no 13 in Colchester's High Street. Earlier, in 1901, there had been plans to link the town with Southend by a light railway system but the proposals never went ahead. (Lens of Sutton)

top'. The livery was dark brown and cream and the current collection was by overhead trolley, which was set to one side of the car. The staircases were reversed and destination boards were fitted high above the front deck rails.

Within a month of opening there were complaints from the local clergy and ministers, who wanted trams suspended during church services on Sundays. This was a common complaint in many towns and included a number of clergymen who were concerned that the noise of the passing trams drowned the words of their sermons. Colchester Corporation held a lively debate on the issue but decided by a small majority that nothing should be done.

Tram routes covered services from North Station to Lexden, East Gates and Hythe. In 1905 Parliament agreed an extension of single track from St Botolph's to the recreation ground. Again trams covered this route from North Station and, to cope with the extra service, two further cars (nos 17 and 18)

Hythe-bound car no 6 descends St Botolph's Street before turning into Magdalen Street. The system never comprised more than 18 cars during its life and no improvements ever took place. (Lens of Sutton)

St Botolph's Street, Colchester, photographed on a wet modern-day afternoon. A number of the buildings from the beginning of the 20th century still exist. (Author)

Colchester car no 3 about to descend North Hill bound for North Station. Because of the 1 in 12 gradient, all Colchester's trams were fitted with track brakes. (Lens of Sutton)

were obtained but built by the United Electric Car Co Ltd. Unlike the earlier cars they had direct staircases. The fleet now comprised a total of 18 cars and no further cars were bought during the system's life.

At the top of Queen Street at the junction with High Street single track was necessary along the curve in the road. To avoid cars meeting, a signalling system was installed, although it was necessary for the driver to switch on the signal when entering the section and switch it off again when leaving. Fares were in 1d sections with a typical cost of 1d to travel from North Station to the top of North Hill.

The trams led a fairly uneventful existence, although there was a problem in 1908 when a car caught the handle of a blind man's barrel organ, turning it over. In consequence the organist sued the corporation for £14 15s, while the latter claimed obstruction. It was finally settled out of court without the corporation admitting liability. Another occasion proved a happier one when car no 10 was highly decorated to carry a wedding party. However, when the 1914–18 war came, the tramway, like many others, suffered problems. The condition of the track grew steadily worse and no work was carried out on any of the cars.

Even after the war no modernisation took place and in 1927 the corporation decided to terminate the system. A Bill was presented to Parliament, which authorised the abandonment of the trams and agreed the operation of trolleybuses on the tramway routes and the use of motor buses elsewhere within the borough. No trolleybuses were ever run in Colchester but a number of offers to operate bus services were received from private companies. However, the corporation decided to go ahead with a scheme of its own to replace the trams with motor buses. Even so a number of private operators ran buses within the borough before the passing of the Act and the fares were generally 50% higher than on the trams.

Over the next two years the sections of tramway gradually gave way to corporation buses. The last tram ran to Lexden on 30th September 1928 and in the summer of 1929 the section between North Station and the top of North Hill was abandoned because of the poor condition of the track. In the same year the corporation agreed that the private bus operators could continue but fares would be charged at the same rate as the corporation buses for all journeys within the borough. In return the private operators paid the corporation 25% of their receipts.

The last tram in Colchester ran on 8th December 1929, by which time all routes were covered by buses. It was not long before most of the rails were lifted although some were covered over as the roads were reinstated. At the same time the tram depot in Magdalen Street was converted for use by buses. The majority of the car bodies were sold to a local builder, who used them as site huts. Some survived to become garden sheds and one of these stood for many years in the garden of a private residence at the village of Great Horkesley, just off the A134 between Colchester and Sudbury. According to R.C. Anderson in his book *The Tramways of East Anglia*, it

The saloon body of a Colchester tram used as a garden shed at a private residence in the village of Great Horkesley. It is believed to be either car no 6 or car no 9. (Author)

could have been the body of either car 6 or car 9, both of which were known to have survived until 1963 at least in local villages. Unfortunately, examination of the body gave no indication of the number although most of the windows and the end doors had remained intact.

At the Magdalen Street depot, sections of tram track can still be seen. The shed carried six roads and when the inspection pits were extended some years ago for use by buses, the depot's director was besieged by enthusiasts who sought sections of the redundant track. The workshop obliged by cutting pieces 6 to 9 inches long for the 'buffs'!

Also some years back, during a clearout at the depot offices, specifications were found amid the dust and dirt dating back to before the start of the trams in 1904. In addition there were copies of engineers' reports to the corporation dated 1927/8, prepared during the proposed change from trams to either trolleybuses or motor buses. The costing was detailed down to the last ½d.

The body of Colchester tram no 13 photographed at Parsons Heath on 12th March 1950. According to local newspaper reports, it spent time after closure of the tramway system as a potting shed at Pondfield Cottage, Harwich Road (close to Parsons Heath), but was ultimately destroyed by fire in the 1960s. (John H. Meredith)

The workshops at the depot once served as stables for horses used at the nearby St Botolph's railway station, which had been brought into use on 1st March 1866 by the Tendring Hundred Railway. In the late 1970s the gulleys under the depot's inspection pits were examined and it was found, to the surprise of all concerned, that a tunnel (now blocked for obvious security reasons) linked the pits with the railway station a hundred yards or so away.

3

East Anglia Transport Museum

Trams preserved at Carlton Colville

London HR/2 tram 1858 passes admiring spectators at Carlton Colville. Built by English Electric in 1930 for use on hilly routes in the capital, it was purchased for preservation in 1952. Prior to its arrival at Carlton Colville, it spent a number of years at Chessington Zoo as a static exhibit. (Roy Makewell)

The East Anglia Transport Museum (EATM) can be found at Carlton Colville not far from the Beccles–Lowestoft road (A146) and just off Chapel Road (B1384). It is open from Easter to the end of September on Sundays and Bank Holidays, plus Wednesdays and Saturdays from June to September, also on weekdays except Mondays during August. A wide range of trams and trolleybuses is exhibited alongside many preserved road vehicles, from motor cars to steam rollers, and a narrow-gauge railway.

The museum was founded on its present site in 1965 when a small band of local enthusiasts was reorganised to become the East Anglia Transport Museum Society. The museum started with just a few vehicles that had already been donated or loaned but there were no other assets. The society faced the task of transforming disused meadows – kindly provided by the society's founder and first chairman, Mr A.V. Bird – into a museum that could be open to the public. Workshops and offices were needed as well as stores, refreshment facilities, toilets and so forth. In addition, if running trams or trolleybuses were ever to be contemplated, roads, track and overhead wires were needed.

Throughout the museum's life the exhibits have been brought together entirely by amateurs, with finance coming mostly from the enthusiasts themselves plus what is spent or donated by visitors. In addition, the majority of the work is carried out by members who give their time completely free of charge. It is to their credit therefore that by the end of 1966 the first buildings were erected, with the first road construction and tram track completed the same year.

On 12th November 1970 development was sufficiently advanced for a tramcar, Blackpool 159, to be operated under its own power for the first time at Carlton Colville. Not long afterwards a London Transport trolleybus made history by being the first to be worked in a museum anywhere in the country.

There was great excitement when, on 24th May 1972, the museum opened to the public. In the same year a narrow-gauge railway was constructed with completion in time for the Whitsun holiday in 1973. It had really become a place for a day out – for all the family. The not-so-young could rekindle memories with the trams and trolleybuses on exhibition and the young could look on in wonder at these strange vehicles of the past. New amenities were gradually added and surely enthusiasts' dreams were realised when, from July 1982, they could take an extended tram ride through woodland to a new terminus at Hedley Grove. In 2001 an adjacent property, Hedley Lodge, was purchased to provide education, library and conference facilities and a car park.

Trams exhibited range from the early open-top double-decker to the sturdier large-capacity city tramcar. An early vehicle is Lowestoft car no 14, superbly restored following the many years it spent as a summerhouse before being 'rescued' in 1961. It is currently being re-restored to get it into an operational condition. The car was built by Milnes in 1904 for the Lowestoft Corporation where it survived until replaced by buses in 1931. It is typical of many trams constructed for use throughout the country early last century. It was originally built for a 3 ft 6 in gauge although its present truck is standard gauge to permit movement on museum track.

Numerous trolleybuses can be found. These include five

This Sunbeam MF2B Weymann-bodied trolleybus served in Bournemouth until 1968. It was later 'rescued' from a scrap merchant for preservation. It is photographed here in the late 1970s. (East Anglia Transport Museum)

The only known tram with gutters and a downspout! The body of this 1904 single-deck Lowestoft tram spent nearly 60 years built into the back of a bungalow in Lowestoft before being acquired by the East Anglia Transport Museum. (Author)

Sunbeam vehicles acquired from various parts of the country, a typical example being Derby trolleybus no 224 operated by Derby Corporation from 1952 to 1967. The popularity of the trolleybus began during the 1930s when it was seen as a more flexible replacement for the tram yet still retaining some of the tram's better features. But they were comparatively short-lived, since in later years the high cost of electricity and the maintenance of the overhead wiring helped to bring about their decline, at a time of cheaply imported crude oil.

There is much more to see at Carlton Colville. Walking the museum's roadway beside its tram tracks seems like a trip back into the past, with items such as Victorian pillar boxes, ornate street lighting columns and road signs, horse troughs and drinking fountains, a shop window displaying many items of yesteryear, plus an example of the first type of public telephone kiosk – complete with 'buttons A and B'. Three tramway junction boxes are to be found, having previously been used as street-side equipment – one by Great Yarmouth Corporation Tramways.

31

One of the latest exhibits at the museum is the body of a single-deck tram from the Lowestoft system. Only four of this type were ever operated in East Anglia, all of them in Lowestoft. This tram, which ran in service from 1904 to 1931, is now painted in the old Lowestoft livery and utilised for the display of small tramway objects.

During the author's visit it was possible to ride two trolleybuses, one from Maidstone and another from London, as well as a London 'HR/2' and a Blackpool standard tram. What more could one ask for a day out with so many exhibits and plenty of space to park the car!

4
Trams Divided By
A Bridge

Great Yarmouth Corporation Tramways

Car no 6 at the market place turning towards Theatre Plain, c1910. The track through the market was relaid and doubled in 1913. (Lens of Sutton)

Great Yarmouth, renowned for many years as a major herring port and today a popular holiday centre, is a long town stretched out over miles of the Norfolk coast. Yet, unlike Lowestoft (see Chapter 6), the tramway system of Great Yarmouth was split into two since the bridge across the river Yare was not suitable for trams. The bridge remained a narrow wooden structure until 1930, with the centre span being raised and lowered by hand winches. However, the

Great Yarmouth's market place, c1922. Car 34 on the right is making for Theatre Plain and Regent Road, while the car on the extreme left from Fish Wharf waits for the preceding car (no 4) to clear. (Pamlin Prints)

towns did share the possibility in 1898 of a light railway system from Caister through Yarmouth and Lowestoft to Southwold but this did not materialise.

Before the arrival of the trams, the only way to get about in Great Yarmouth, apart from walking or by cab, was by a vehicle known as Limmer's omnibus, which regularly plied between Feather's Plain and the Buck Inn. When the first tramway came in April 1875 it was a horse-operated system that offered a service from Southtown railway station to Feather's Plain at Gorleston. Later a summer service was extended to Brush Quay. The gauge was 4 ft 8½ ins and the rails were laid on wooden sleepers. Yet there was opposition to the trams, especially from the cab drivers. One night during the construction of the track a strong party of roughs overcame the watchman and threw a number of rails into the river from the Bollard Quay.

The horse trams ran at 15-minute intervals but the going was slow. It was reported that the journey was as 'pleasant

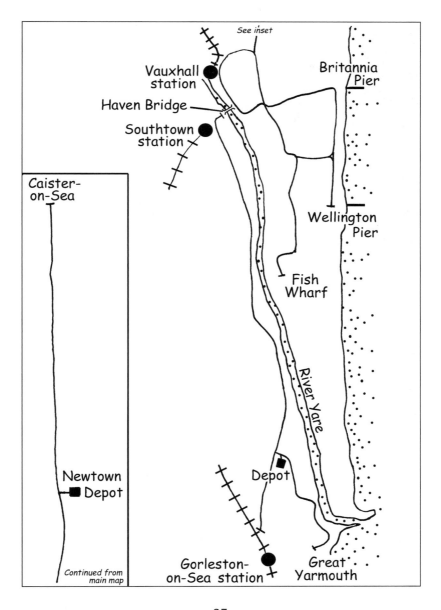

and easy as one could desire'. First class passengers were given the innermost seats just behind the driver with the additional amenity of having 'extra straw to keep the feet warm in wintry weather'. Despite such 'comfort' it could take up to 2½ hours to complete a single journey. There had earlier been plans to reach as far south as Halesworth – one shudders to think how long such a ride might have taken.

In 1878 the company was acquired by the Yarmouth & Gorleston Tramways Co, which in 1882 relaid the track in concrete and to a gauge of 3 ft 6 ins. By this time the fleet consisted of ten horse-drawn double-deck cars, each capable of seating 46 people. In addition, the company operated a number of double-deck horse buses. Despite several extensions being added, the route length only ever reached just over 3 miles. A depot was built at Gorleston plus stables that could accommodate the 68 horses.

In the years that followed, the company suffered financially with the shareholders losing some £17,500. In 1896 pressure was growing for a municipal tramway and in 1898 the corporation successfully applied for Parliamentary powers to construct its own electric tramway. Competition came in 1900 from the British Electric Traction Company (BET), which acquired the horse tram company at less than 75% of its par value but its various attempts to apply for powers to electrify the system were vetoed by the corporation, which was going ahead anyway with its own system. Meantime, because of general demand, steel prices had risen and no further action was taken until the autumn of 1901 when the corporation invited quotations for the supply of rails. The successful company came from Belgium with its offer far lower than any British firm.

Work began on 16th October 1901 on a complex of lines from the Caister Road depot. This included a route to Marine Parade reaching Wellington Pier and a branch to Vauxhall railway station returning via the quays and Regent Street. The gauge was 3 ft 6 ins and the overhead line system was used. A Board of Trade inspection was carried out on 19th June 1902

Great Yarmouth's Town Hall and Quay not long after electric trams began in June 1902. The track on the right-hand side of the road served Great Eastern Railway trains on a branch to Fish Wharf. (Lens of Sutton)

when the tramway was passed as suitable for public service. That afternoon three cars, suitably decorated, toured the crowded route. One of the cars must have been quite a spectacle for it carried on its top deck the band of the Prince of Wales' Own Norfolk Artillery. The following day, Friday, 20th June 1902, a full public service was available.

The first batch of 14 cars arrived for the opening from Brush of Loughborough. These were four-window open-top four-wheeled vehicles, each seating 56 passengers and equipped with two 25 hp motors. The lower deck had longitudinal seats while 'on top' they were wooden reversible garden-type seats. The livery was maroon and cream and the corporation's coat of arms was displayed on the centre of the maroon upper side panel with the words 'Gt. Yarmouth Corporation Tramways' on the cream rocker panel.

Short extensions to the route were added in 1904/5. There were also plans to build a subway under the river Yare or

Services between Haven Bridge and Gorleston began on 4th July 1905 although the bridge was never crossed and the town's tramway remained in two parts throughout. A car passes the Quay, making for Gorleston Beach, c1910. (Lens of Sutton)

The Quay at Gorleston in September 1990. The route between Southtown and Gorleston closed in September 1930 after only 25 years of service although trams survived on the northern section to Caister until December 1933. (Author)

38

alternatively rebuild the river bridge but nothing was done and not at any time did trams cross the river. In September 1905 a decision was taken to widen the bridge but again nothing came of it. Trams commenced services from Haven Bridge to Gorleston on 4th July 1905 and the two parts of the town's tramway system remained divided throughout.

To operate the Gorleston section, ten new open-top cars were supplied, again from Brush, and a further two allocated to north of the bridge. The opening of the Gorleston section meant of course the end of the horse trams so an auction was held at Southtown's Yareside Stables. The horses were sold at prices reaching 35 guineas and a number of trams were sold off to private residents at prices ranging between 8 and 10½ guineas. Some of the better known horses had acquired names such as 'Polly', 'Smasher', 'Bess' or even 'Lopsy Popsy'.

An extension, opened in the northern section, reached Fish Wharf on 8th August 1905 and during 1906 five further cars were purchased from Brush. When a final major extension to cross the borough boundary to Caister opened on 16th May 1907 the systems were virtually complete, with almost 10 route miles of track. To meet the extra demand, now Caister's developing sea front and cemetery were reached, four further Brush cars were acquired, making a total of 35 in all. Trams on the Southtown to Gorleston route provided a 15-minute service in the winter, improved to every 7½ minutes in the summer months and carrying many passengers on to Gorleston Beach. On the northern section trams ran between Wellington Pier and Caister every 15 minutes. Colour signals protected four sections of single track and 'Next Car' clocks were installed at three locations. In addition, ten 'waiting shelters' were erected along the route.

The First World War brought the problems experienced by most tramway undertakings, with shortages of parts and staff. No new cars were purchased and most of the cash available went on repairs and track replacements. In 1920 the Tramway Committee decided to consider motor buses with the result that three second-hand open-top double-deck vehicles were

Car 13 passes along Marine Parade bound for Wellington Pier. As motor buses were introduced during the 1920s so tram routes were closed. The last tram between Vauxhall station and Wellington Pier ran on 6th October 1929. (Lens of Sutton)

purchased from the London General Omnibus Co Ltd for £1,725. A bus service began on 20th October 1920 to support the existing tram service on routes between Vauxhall station and Wellington Pier. The buses carried advertisements, one of these ironically reading 'Travel by Tram'.

The introduction of buses led to the abandonment of tram services from Newtown to Fish Wharf on 14th May 1924. On that day trams also stopped running along St Peter's Road as well as along Fullers Hill between Vauxhall station and Church Plain. Track renewal also became necessary elsewhere, causing heavy financial commitments on the undertaking. As further buses were introduced during the late 1920s, so the tram service from Vauxhall station to Wellington Pier terminated on 6th October 1929.

When closure of the tram service from Southtown to Gorleston was announced in May 1930 there were immediate

40

questions. 'What will happen to the crowds who packed the trams when there will only be limited accommodation on the buses?' some wondered. The Tramway Committee said they would do their best until further buses arrived. 'But what are the folk with infants going to do?' asked the mothers who had often been able to leave their prams on the driver's platform. A wit unkindly suggested the buses could tow the prams behind them. When the final journey came on 25th September 1930, car no 17 was used. This was the same car that made the first trip when the line was first electrified in July 1905.

During 1931 local inhabitants were surprised to see a trolleybus operating experimentally between Yarmouth and Caister. It was a Garrett single-deck vehicle, which for the occasion used one trolley on the overhead wire with the earth return being a 'skate' trailing along behind in the tramway rail. This unusual practice had previously been used on a regular basis in Birmingham where trolleybuses had to use tram-only routes to reach the depot. There the skate resembled and acquired the nickname of 'a string of sausages'. At Yarmouth it was thought that the corporation might proceed with trolleybuses but the idea never materialised.

As the number of motor buses increased so the end of the tramway system came nearer. It survived until 14th December 1933 when car no 6 made the final journey from the market place to the depot. The car was driven by Mayor Peter Ellis, the conductor was Alderman Arthur Beevor and other council members were passengers. Many onlookers were present and to mark the occasion fog detonators exploded on the track. After tea in the mess room, the Chairman of the Transport Committee made a closing speech during which he said that had Shakespeare been present he might have declaimed:

'Farewell, old tram, no more can you be mended;
    Go rest in peace
Your useful life has ended.'

Many of the cars finished their lives as holiday chalets at a

Caister holiday camp and it was not long before most of the rails had gone. The tracks at the Caister Road depot were covered some years ago and the depot now serves Great Yarmouth Transport buses. Above the depot entrance the various stages of travel are depicted – the Rocket, a coach and a bus. At Gorleston the past is remembered by the Tramway Inn, with a signboard showing a Great Yarmouth tram. The site of the old horse tram depot that once stood nearby is today occupied by the public library.

Reminders of the past still continue to be found. At the East Anglia Transport Museum at Carlton Colville there is a pre-First World War junction box that had earlier stood in the town's streets in its heavy cast iron cabinet. Also, towards the end of October 1989 the *Great Yarmouth Mercury* reported that, whilst digging along Caister Road, workmen unearthed fragments of old tramlines beneath the road – bringing with them memories of the system that was abandoned some 56 years previously.

5
Narrow Trams For Narrow Streets

Ipswich Corporation Tramways

A tram negotiates King Street bound for Cornhill, c1906. Note the absence of any other traffic – hardly possible today! (Lens of Sutton)

A visit to the old Priory Heath bus depot in Ipswich's Cobham Road not too long ago truly seemed a trip into the past. In pride of place for a tram enthusiast was the saloon body of double-deck open-top tramcar no 33 on a loader near the entrance. Built by Brush of Loughborough in 1904, it had survived the years well despite the fact that a good part of its life was spent as a store shed at Claydon, a village just north of

Inside car no 33 at the Ipswich Transport Museum. Built in 1904, the car is in pretty fair condition. It was found in use as a store shed at Claydon. (Author)

the town. Car no 33's three main windows on each side were intact and the words 'Ipswich Corporation Tramways' could just be determined on the side. There was also evidence of the gold lining on some of the platform panels. A notice inside the saloon read 'Do not tender gold coins'.

The Priory Heath depot began life in 1936 housing trolleybuses but when it closed in 1987 it was accommodating motor buses. For a time it was used as a paint shop and work shop. Following transfer of these facilities to Constantine Road, Priory Heath was used by various council departments and also as a store for the developing Ipswich Transport Museum. Following several successful open days the council agreed to lease the entire depot to the museum, which opened its doors to the public in time for Easter 1995.

Another delight to be found is the oldest known trolleybus fully restored to its original livery. ICT trolleybus no 2, DX 3988, was built in 1923, the body by Shorts of Rochester and

Ipswich's oldest known trolleybus DX 3988, built in 1923, has been fully restored to its original livery. It can be seen at the Ipswich Transport Museum. (Author)

the chassis by Railless Ltd. It has not quite been restored to its former state for it previously had an open-backed end for smokers. It is interesting to recall that the people of Ipswich called their trolleybuses 'trams' at a time when elsewhere they were referred to as 'trolleys'. With Ipswich an early operator of electric buses, they were regarded as 'trackless trams'.

Another aspect of the past once existed in Quadling Street, not far from the railway station. When visited in September 1990 tracks leading into the yard could be seen, tracks that were once used by horse trams. But the wooden depot that housed the trams was no longer there. Because it had become unsafe, it had been removed to the Cobham Road depot piece by piece by Manpower Services and stored pending restoration. Each piece of wood had been carefully labelled and the original site extensively photographed so that hopefully one day the shed could be rebuilt. Later the whole area was

Horse tram tracks in evidence at the Quadling Street depot when visited in September 1990. Sadly all this has gone, with the site now comprising a major leisure development of cinema, bars and night clubs. (Author)

levelled and incorporated into a major leisure development including a cinema, bars and nightclubs. A sad ending for an historic site. The remaining lengths of track and stone setts were removed to the Transport Museum where, one day, they may be reunited with a reconstructed depot.

Horse trams came to Ipswich to meet the needs of a rapidly growing population. A gauge of 3 ft 6 ins was chosen and the first line was constructed in the spring of 1880 from Cornhill to the railway station. The opening was delayed because after completion the contractor had been declared bankrupt. The first tramcar, a single-deck car built by Starbuck of Birkenhead, arrived in August 1880 and the Mayor and Town Clerk were passengers on a trial run. During its journey it came off the rails – much to the amusement of the local cabbies, who viewed the trams as potential rivals.

The grand opening came on Wednesday, 13th October 1880.

The fare was 2d, which passengers dropped into a locked tin box, and the journey was comparatively comfortable since red velvet cushions were provided. At first there were two single-deck four-wheeled cars, which had to be stored at either end of the line when not in use. Land for a yard was not obtained until several days later, on 18th October 1880, and the Quadling Street depot was not constructed until 1883. The livery was maroon and cream with the name 'Ipswich Tramway Company' on the rocker panels.

In March 1881 horse trams were reaching Brooks Hall Road via Portman Road and Norwich Road. Their popularity was undoubted since over 1,000 passengers were carried on the Easter Monday Bank Holiday of that year. To meet increased demand, two further cars were ordered, one a four-wheeled double-deck car, open-topped with back-to-back (knifeboard) seating along the centre. The following year a route between Barrack Corner and Cornhill was opened, which meant that cars to Brooks Hall Road could run via Cornhill. When trams reached Derby Road station in the summer of 1883 the service was complete. To cover this route two double-deck cars were each hauled by two horses but with a third horse attached to pull the car up the hill at St John's Road. By the mid-1880s the tramway company owned eight cars and eighteen horses to cover the four miles of track.

In 1893 the horse trams were withdrawn from service for two weeks because the company refused to accept the corporation's terms for repairing the roads. The wood paving between the rails had deteriorated badly, particularly in Westgate Street and St Matthew's Street. Since tramway companies under an Act of 1870 were held responsible for the condition of the roadway between the rails and up to 18 ins each side of the track, the corporation had served notice for the work to be done. The repair bill came to £832 and the corporation eventually agreed to carry out the work against payment by the company of £100 per year, after which services were resumed. During the trams' absence, local cab proprietors were of course quick to take advantage of the situation. Despite the company's problems, a further double-deck car was purchased in 1896 for £158 and three single-deck cars were converted to double-deckers.

On 20th June 1898 Ipswich saw bright red horse-drawn buses on its streets, offering cheap fares and frequent journeys. They were known locally as the 'Penny Omnibuses' and they were able to cover new routes, thus competing strongly with the trams. In addition the buses ran on Sundays, which the trams never had done. The tramway company retaliated by reducing its fares but its finances remained very strained. Attempts by the company to sell its concern to another company proved unsuccessful and in 1901 the corporation served a compulsory purchase order allowed under the 1870 Tramways Act. The price was eventually settled by arbitration at £17,552. The corporation took over the responsibility of running the horse trams from 1st November 1901. They lasted only until 6th June 1903 when, hardly a financial success, they ceased running to make way for electric trams in the town.

The authority to provide this 'new form of traction' came with the passing of the Ipswich Corporation Tramways Act 1900. As soon as the horse trams stopped, the old rails were lifted which meant that no trams ran for several months. This provided a haven for the horse-bus operators although the widespread roadworks gave many problems. Meantime the horse trams were sold off to become shepherd's huts and chicken sheds and the like.

A major consideration in deciding to maintain the gauge of 3 ft 6 ins was the town's narrow streets. In addition there were many curves, particularly one at Major's Corner with a radius of 40 ft, although gradients were not severe. The permanent-way construction was carried out by Dick, Kerr & Co Ltd, providing in all 10.82 route miles at a cost of £41,220. To commence the service 26 double-deck open-top Brush cars were acquired, each powered by two 25 hp Westinghouse motors. Current collection was from overhead wires and the cars were painted dark green and cream, outlined in gold and black, with the fleet number on each dash. In the centre of the

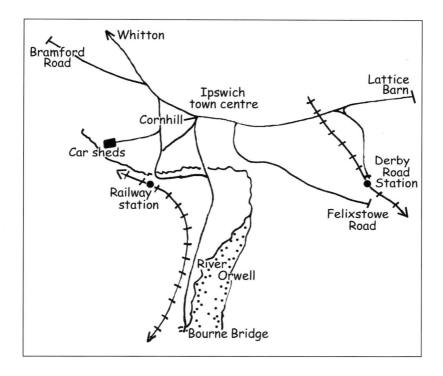

waist panel was the corporation crest and on the rocker panel was written 'Ipswich Corporation Tramways'. A feature of the cars was that they had an overall width of 5 ft 9 ins, making them at the time the narrowest used in this country.

The weather was poor for the official opening on 21st November 1903 when Mrs Bennett, the Mayoress, opened the main doorway at the tramway offices with a silver key to declare the Ipswich Corporation Tramways open. A civic lunch was held in the specially decorated repair shop after which the guests were given a special tour to Whitton. Many local residents turned out to watch these 'five cars aglow with electric lights'. Unfortunately a number of minor mishaps occurred around the time the service began. On a trial run at

49

Bourne Bridge car no 8 passes the Wolsey Pharmacy at the junction of St Nicholas Street and Silent Street, c1910. (Lens of Sutton)

The same scene in September 1990. The Wolsey Pharmacy has become an international firm of auctioneers and valuers and the trams (and the trolleybuses) have long since gone. (Author)

night on 10th November 1903 car no 22 had left the rails because of a faulty point setting. On the day public services began, Monday, 23rd November, car no 20 left the rails at the top of Princes Street and it took two further cars to get it right again. The following day there was a power failure, but after this such misfortunes became rare.

The trams were immediately popular and crowds gathered at Cornhill to watch them pass. On the first day the only route open was from Whitton to Bourne Bridge (via Cornhill and Ipswich station) together with a spur off Wherstead Road along Bath Street to reach the river steamers. Further routes to Lattice Barn, Derby Road station and along Bramford Road followed on 21st December, on which date the 'Penny Omnibuses' were discontinued. In May 1904 the system was completed when trams reached the Royal Oak via Bishops Hill and Felixstowe Road. To meet the extra demand ten further open-topped Brush cars were ordered, making 36 in all.

Trams at the Ipswich Great Eastern Railway station not long after the system opened. From the picture it looks as though the trolley arm (just out of the picture) has come off the overhead wire. (Colin Withey collection)

51

An early picture of car no 21 passing the Social Settlement building on the Wherstead Road route. (Lens of Sutton)

Fares ranged from ld to 3d with tickets being the Bell punch type, cancelled at the printed stages by hand-operated punches. Ipswich Corporation also sold books of pre-paid tickets, which were exchanged during travel for an ordinary ticket of the same value. Tram stops, familiar to many towns, were clearly marked as 'Fare Stage', 'Cars stop if required' or 'All Cars Stop'. In August 1905 half-fares were introduced before 8 am.

The First World War meant staff shortages, as with all transport systems, and spare parts were virtually unobtainable. With paint soon in short supply, a number of cars were painted grey overall. Ten were affected but only one (no 36) returned to its original livery at a later date. The remaining cars, painted grey, were used on special workmen's services. In 1917 the short branch along Bath Street was closed and the rails removed since new track could not be purchased. The poles remained to distribute electricity to the local houses.

After the war the track was in a badly worn state, partly due

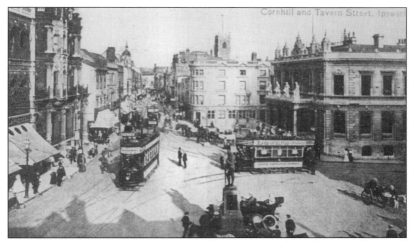

Cornhill and Tavern Street, c1910. Electric trams lasted in Ipswich until July 1926 when they were replaced by trolleybuses. (Lens of Sutton)

to the heavy industrial traffic that passed through the town's narrow streets during wartime. Much of the damage had been caused by horse-drawn vehicles with metal tyres. Due to the heavy costs for renewal there was soon a call to 'scrap the trams'. At the same time Thomas Tilling motor buses had started services although their licence stipulated a minimum fare within the borough to protect the trams.

Certain tracks were relaid in 1921 when rails were again available but ideas to end the trams persisted. As a result of this, Ipswich Corporation hired three Railless/English Electric trolleybuses, which commenced services between Cornhill and Ipswich station on 2nd September 1923. Consequently the trams along the route ceased operation but since overhead wires already existed, only an additional negative wire was needed. The trolleybuses were two-motor single-deck vehicles, each with 30 seats, which included eight in an open-ended compartment at the rear for smokers. The trolleybuses worked as pay-as-you-enter vehicles and were one-man-operated.

The trolleybuses proved successful so the three vehicles were purchased. The track in Princes Street was removed and the road resurfaced. Ipswich Corporation had become one of the first in the country to convert a route from tram to trolleybus operation. When a fourth single-deck trolleybus was acquired in 1924 it was made by Ransomes, Sims & Jefferies, an Ipswich company. The Eastern Counties Road Car Co Ltd (previously Thomas Tilling) was, not unexpectedly, concerned at the potential competition and offered to provide a fleet of motor buses to the corporation. In addition the company stated its willingness to pay the corporation £6,000 a year for 20 years in return for the four trolleybuses and it also sought protection against competition from the trams. The council was not happy about the offer so a referendum was held. The ratepayers decided by 3,780 votes to 2,156 votes to keep the trolleybuses so, during 1925, another single-deck experimental vehicle was purchased.

The former tram depot at Constantine Road is today used by Ipswich buses. The old tram tracks were taken out as recently as 1987 and filled over. (Author)

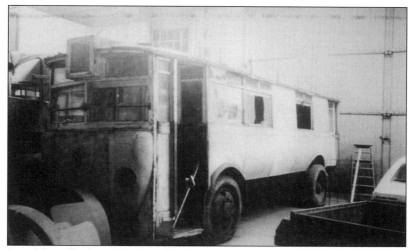

Ipswich trolleybus DX 8871 built by Ransomes, Sims & Jefferies in 1930, now owned by the National Museum of Science and Industry, is currently stored at Wroughton, near Swindon. (Author)

Ipswich Corporation applied for Royal Assent to replace its trams by trolleybuses and this was received on 7th August 1925. After a final experimental vehicle, a Ransomes dual-entrance single-decker, was received, the corporation was able to consider which makes to purchase. Gradually the tramway routes were taken over and when the last car ran on 26th July 1926 the conversion was complete. The corporation was operating with 15 Ransomes single-deck dual-entrance trolley-buses and 15 similar Garrett vehicles. The electric trams at Ipswich had served for less than 23 years.

In the early 1930s the experimental vehicles were with-drawn and the first double-deck trolleybuses were introduced. In 1936 the depot at Priory Heath opened serving trolleybuses, which were to survive on many of the town's streets until August 1963. When vehicle no 114 made a last journey to the depot it carried the letters RIP painted on its side.

Apart from the 1923 trolleybus surviving in the Ipswich Transport Museum, there are also five others. A 1926 all Ransomes single-deck vehicle (no 9) lives there plus its Garrett counterpart (no 26) although the latter is still owned by the Long Shop Museum Trust of Leiston, Suffolk. The first Ipswich double-deck trolleybus, another all Ransomes affair from 1933 (no 46), survives in store after an adventurous life as a residential caravan. Later double-decker no 105 (a 1947 Karrier W originally with wooden slatted seats) is also in store but the very last trolleybus purchased by Ipswich is on display. This is a 1950 Sunbeam F4 (no 126) with Park Royal bodywork covered in that mottled aluminium panelling, an Ipswich speciality. Only one other Ipswich trolleybus survives, a 1930 all Ransomes single-deck vehicle (no 44) now owned by the National Museum of Science and Industry and stored at Wroughton, near Swindon.

6
Trams Across A
Swing Bridge

Lowestoft Corporation Tramways

Car no 8 in Lowestoft's London Road not long after the tramway system began in 1903. The town's trams lasted almost 28 years. (Lens of Sutton)

There was excitement among tram enthusiasts at the end of 1988 when a Lowestoft bungalow was put up for sale. Built into the back of the bungalow was discovered the body of a 1904 vintage tram in an excellent state of preservation for its age. The single-deck car, one of only four built, was originally in service between 1904 and 1931 after which it was sold off to become a garden chalet. During that time it acquired a professionally-built pitched roof and it was well painted to protect it from all weathers.

The bungalow's new owner happily agreed to part with the tram body, so in January 1990 it was carefully winched onto a low-loader after which it was slowly transported to a new resting place at the East Anglia Transport Museum at Carlton Colville. The removal had been no easy task. All means had been considered including a possible lift by helicopter but this would have proved very costly. Finally the hauliers, V.C. Cooke & Sons Ltd of Beccles, proved very helpful by lifting the body and carrying it to the museum. The tram body is currently in use as an exhibition room (see Chapter 3).

The single-deck tram body is not the only relic from Lowestoft's tramways. Another tram at Carlton Colville is car no 14, which was rescued for preservation in 1961. This is a double-deck open-topped car built by Milnes in 1904 for the

Lowestoft car no 14 resides today at the East Anglia Transport Museum at Carlton Colville. Built by Milnes in 1904, it spent many years as a summerhouse after its 'retirement' before being restored to its present fine condition. (Author)

A view of the upper deck of Lowestoft 14 at Carlton Colville. Travelling 'on top' was only for the sturdy during wintry weather! (Author)

town's 3 ft 6 in gauge tramway. It spent many years as a summerhouse before being restored, and is currently being re-restored to get it into operational condition. The car's present truck is standard gauge to allow operation on the museum's track (see also Chapter 3).

Trams were first considered in Lowestoft when the Yarmouth & Gorleston Tramways Company obtained powers to build and work a horse-tramway system within the borough but the scheme never materialised. Just before the turn of the century in 1898 the East Anglian Light Railway Company (EALR), a subsidiary of Drake & Gorham Electric Power & Traction Co Ltd, proposed a chain of electric tramways to run from Caister to Great Yarmouth and Lowestoft and then through Kessingland to Southwold. Lowestoft council supported the idea but only agreeing a route from Gorleston via Lowestoft to Kessingland.

Lengthy negotiations between the EALR and Lowestoft council took place and it was eventually decided that the

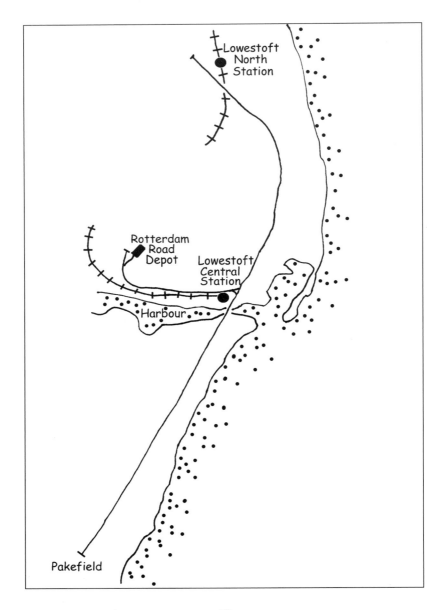

council should itself obtain powers to construct and work an electric tramway from the northern boundary to the southern boundary of the borough. Although the council took over the EALR's powers to extend to Kessingland, the section southwards from Pakefield was never built.

Construction work began in 1903 after a lengthy delay in delivery of the rails, brought in a German tug towed across the North Sea from Antwerp. Much of the 3 ft 6 in gauge track was single with passing places and current collection was by the conventional overhead wire system. The total route length came to just over four miles, running from Yarmouth Road to the north via the High Street and London Road to cross the swing bridge. To the south the trams travelled along London Road South to reach the terminus at a junction with Florence Road at Pakefield. Trams reached a depot built in Rotterdam Road by a branch along Denmark Street from the main route. A service along this short section existed for a time but this was withdrawn after three weeks through lack of demand.

Construction work to allow the crossing by trams of the 40 ft swing bridge, erected by the Great Eastern Railway in 1897, proved complicated. When the bridge opened, using its hydraulic power, it first tilted then swung upon a pivot. For this reason the tramway overhead-line equipment had to be built so that it swung with the bridge as one unit. As a precaution a system was incorporated so that when the bridge opened, the overhead line on the bridge and for a suitable distance each side automatically cut out. Catch points were also installed and barriers were placed across the approach. With such devices it was apparent that no tram could approach the bridge when it was open for shipping.

Following the supply of eleven four-wheel open-top double-deck cars and four bogie single-deck cars, all from Milnes, trial tests began over the route. These happened at night giving, it was claimed, disturbed sleep for residents living nearby. However, their troubles were short-lived for inspection of the system by the Board of Trade soon followed and the grand opening day was fixed for Wednesday, 22nd July 1903. The

Car no 12 seen here at Pier Terrace on the section south of the swing bridge. When introduced the trams were immediately popular and in the first two weeks 165,900 passengers were carried. (Colin Withey collection)

Mayor and Mayoress were present for the occasion with many invitations sent out to make up the official party. The first tram was bedecked with flags and evergreens, with flowers festooned around the windows. When it left the depot shortly after noon, many people lined the decorated route. It was the first of a procession of four cars, which travelled to the Yarmouth Road terminus, then south to Pakefield and finally back to the Grand Hotel where the party celebrated with an official lunch.

The system was then opened to the public with a seven minute service in operation. It was well patronised with 165,900 passengers carried in the first two weeks. In 1904 four more double-deck cars were purchased, again from Milnes, giving the fleet its maximum of 19 cars in all, plus a Brush sweeper/sprinkler. Their livery was described as Munich lake and cream but the works car was painted grey. Four of the cars were single-deckers capable of seating 50 passengers and

London Road, c1906, before the age of the motor car. The town's fleet comprised at most fifteen double-deck and four single-deck cars. (Lens of Sutton)

equipped with an open smoking compartment at each end. They were not regularly used, being known as 'winter cars' and they also had an unfortunate tendency to derail on sharp bends.

Despite the trams' initial popularity, all did not go well in the years that followed, largely because of troubles experienced with road foundations. A lot of money had to be spent on repair work. In 1910, through lack of passengers, it was necessary to terminate the northern end at North Parade instead of along Yarmouth Road. In addition the through 1d fare was increased to 2d with 1d stages introduced. In 1912 the condition of the track had deteriorated to the extent that a thorough renovation was necessary. This cost the council £10,000, which had to be borrowed over a fifteen year period. By 1913 the tramway had built up a deficit of £26,000 and fares were raised once again.

The First World War saw the usual shortage of male

Car no 13 seen here at the Pakefield terminus. The car was built in 1904 by G.F. Milnes & Co. (Colin Withey collection)

employees, so women drivers, conductors and inspectors were introduced. As with other systems, materials for maintenance were also in short supply. Yet around that time there were two amusing happenings regarding animals. Just before the First World War a car approached a stop and waiting to get on was an Italian circus master with a dancing bear. The conductor was not happy about having a bear in his car but, after consultation with the driver, it was agreed they could travel on the top deck with the animal considered in the same category as a dog. Immediately all the other passengers fled downstairs.

The second incident occurred a short time after the war. A circus promoter asked if a baby elephant could be carried by tram from Pakefield to the town centre. The tramway manager agreed to this so the car floor was strengthened and the elephant was carried for the normal adult fare of 2d!

In 1920 poles and span wires were installed along Rotterdam Road and Normanston Drive in anticipation of trolleybus operation but no overhead wires were ever erected. The corporation had obtained powers to operate trolleybuses and motor buses earlier that year with plans that trolleybuses should reach new areas including Oulton. In the end only a corporation bus service was introduced – and then not until 1927 when a sea-front service began. The few poles and span wires erected for the trolleybuses were used to support overhead lighting. The motor buses operated what became known as a 'sea wall' service with open saloons available throughout the summer at half-hourly intervals. A poster of the day read:

Lowestoft Corporation Transport.
Motor Omnibus Service will run daily
By the Silvery Sea.

In 1928 the bus service was extended to cover further areas and in 1929 a half-hourly bus service was introduced along the tramway route and beyond to reach the northern borough boundary. It was becoming apparent that the trams were outliving their usefulness and in 1930 the corporation decided to abandon the system in favour of motor buses rather than re-equip and extend the line. On 10th April 1931 removal of the track on the northern section began while trams continued for a time to cover the section to Pakefield.

The last tram in Lowestoft ran on 8th May 1931, driven by the oldest driver, who had served the tramway since it began in 1903. As with the system's inauguration, large crowds turned out but this time the final car carried a huge wreath of lilies heavily bordered and crossed with black. Lowestoft could be proud of its tramway service. It lasted almost 28 years and during that time carried some 80 million passengers with a car mileage of around 8 million miles!

7
Steep Gradients In A Cathedral City

Norwich Electric Tramways Company

Car no 38 passes St Giles church, c1906. The buildings have long since gone and the area is now a roundabout and dual carriageway. (Lens of Sutton)

The City of Norwich covers approximately 15½ square miles but fortunately for the visitor much of its charm is confined to an area of less than 2 square miles. Its well-known castle and cathedral date back to Norman times and its medieval Guildhall was built 80 years before Columbus discovered America!

Inevitably Norwich has many museums. One of these is the Mustard Shop in Royal Arcade where visitors can recall the past in evocative surroundings. Colman's first began making 'Penny Oval' tins of mustard in 1886 when quantities of either 12 or 13 drams of fine mustard were sold – dependent upon how well the company was doing. It seems that in that century a penny went a long way. In 1899 Mr E.B. Southwell, a former manager and director of J. & J. Colman Ltd. said: 'The Penny Tin pays everybody. The penny pays the farmer who grows the seed, the railway company, the cost of manufacture, making the tin, printing the label, weighing and filling, despatching, the wholesaler's profit, the grocer's profit, and everybody is satisfied – including the customer who gets a supply of excellent mustard for his humble penny.'

Also in Norwich is the Bridewell Museum of Norwich Trade and Industries. Exhibits range from a colourful textiles display to the splendour of a steam fire engine, and a scale model of a tram is prominently displayed. This was made around 1960 by the late Russell Gamble of Norwich and donated to the museum by Mrs P. Gamble in 1987. The exhibit, complete with traction poles and overhead wire, is of car no 35 with its destination board reading 'Earlham Road and Thorpe Road'. The museum's other tramway exhibits include numerous tickets, badges and buttons, a tram driver's cap, a destination board, portfolio plans for the city dating from the 1890s and a 3 ft section of rail recovered from St Andrews Street.

The first public transport system in Norwich comprised a horse-drawn bus service provided by the Norwich Omnibus Company Ltd, which began between Thorpe railway station and Dereham Road on 23rd June 1879. Other routes ran from Newmarket Road to Catton at the Whalebone public house, Unthank Road to Bracondale and from Earlham Road to Thorpe Village. The vehicles were single-deckers with the driver's seat high up. The driver collected the fares through a trap door set in the roof. On the route from Thorpe station to Thorpe Gardens, double-deckers were used with knifeboard seating on top.

Car no 11 on the Thorpe Road and Newmarket Road service passes the Fountain, c1906 which was situated at the junction of Newmarket Road and Ipswich Road. (Colin Withey collection)

Prior to the buses there had been applications for tramway systems but these had not materialised. In 1883 a cable tramway was proposed by Andrew Hallidie, an American from San Francisco. The idea was that a cable running in a conduit between the rails would be attached to a car by a controllable gripper with the cable wound on and off a drum at the cable station. The scheme was considered by the Norwich City Council's Parliamentary and By-Laws Committee, which decided that the construction and working of the system would cause significant 'nuisance and discomfort'. Accordingly the company gave up its proposal, although it is worth noting that Hallidie's cable trams still operate in San Francisco even though mainly as a tourist attraction.

Two further schemes came and went. In 1886 the Norwich Tramways Company Ltd was brought into existence and a Tramways Order was granted the following year. Despite this, the company gave up the idea in December 1889. Seven years later in 1896 the British Electric Traction Company (BET) proposed a company to be known as the Norwich and

District Light Railways which would build a network of light railways to connect as far afield as Hingham to the west and Bungay and Beccles to the south-east. However, this was not to be and it was the Norwich Electric Tramways Company, incorporated by the New General Traction Company, that finally gained the City Council's consent. A Bill was approved by Parliament on 20th July 1897 and in February 1898 the City Council gave the go-ahead for work to commence and in 1899 horse buses ceased operations.

Considerable street improvements were necessary before the tracks could be laid. There were many narrow streets, numerous curves and some steep gradients with the steepest at 1 in 14.5. Certain streets had to be widened and a new street had to be cut on St Andrews Hill through the buildings in Redwell Street. An ironmongers' shop on Orford Hill had to be demolished. There was much hard bargaining over the various construction costs and it was eventually agreed that this should be shared between the company and the council. As far as the company was concerned, this was in addition to its expected responsibility under the 1870 Tramways Act to repair the tramway and the roadway between the rails and 18 inches on each side. The gauge was 3 ft 6 ins and over 15 route miles were built. Overhead wires were used for the 550v DC current collection. The current for the overhead wires came from a two-storey brick power station in Duke Street constructed by the tramway company. The depot and repair shops were sited in Silver Street where all 50 cars could be accommodated.

Just over three years after Parliamentary approval, the grand opening came. On 30th July 1900 the electric trams commenced services on four routes in the city. Crowds lined the streets to watch and it is said that men being shaved left their chairs with lather on their faces to stand and stare at the trams as they 'clanged and swished' past them. The success of the trams was undoubted. Routes included Magdalen Road, Earlham Road, Dereham Road and Thorpe Road. Other routes opened later that year included Aylsham Road, Mousehold

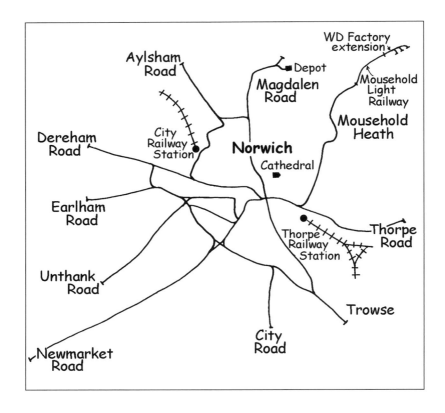

Heath, Newmarket Road, City Road and Trowse. By the end of the year a further route opened along Unthank Road. At first all services operated to and from the Tramway Centre at Orford Place with its circular waiting room. The centre soon became very congested so that from April 1901 cross-city services were introduced on most routes. In 1904 the track at Orford Place was relaid, thus further easing the situation.

The initial fleet consisted of 50 cars, comprising 40 motor cars and 10 trailer cars. They were all double-deck open-top four-wheel cars mounted on Peckham Cantilever trucks with 30 inch diameter wheels. Most of the cars were equipped with

Cars 40 and 16 pass at the Royal Hotel end of Castle Meadow with the picture looking down Prince of Wales Road. Car no 16 was one of five sold to Coventry in 1910. (Lens of Sutton)

Looking down Prince of Wales Road, September 1990. The last tram passed along this street nearly 70 years ago. (Author)

two Westinghouse 25 hp motors although a number had 30 hp motors. The bodies, built by the Brush Electrical Engineering Company, had seating for 52 passengers with an equal number inside or on top. Inside, the seats were longitudinal with rugs for upholstery, whereas on the top deck garden-type seats with covers were used. The livery was maroon and ivory and the trailer cars were used mostly on the service to Trowse and to Mousehold when traffic was heavy.

Life was hard for the staff at such times. A conductor was paid 3d an hour but a motorman did better at 4d an hour. Services on all routes started between 6.30 am and 7 am but with a later start on Sundays. There was no guaranteed week and there were no holidays. Rules were strict with conditions laid down. For example, any crews backing a car without reversing the trolley rendered themselves liable to dismissal.

Norwich's tramways had a rather unusual ticket issuing system. The conductor had a cylindrical canister (about the size of the one pound cocoa tin of the day), painted black and containing a spool on which he slid rolls of tickets. Each roll was separated by a circular piece of cardboard and the tickets projected through a slot in the canister. They were torn off as required and then punched by a hand machine to cancel and register the number issued. It was a system used in Coventry where the tramway company was also a New General Traction Company subsidiary.

In 1909 Norwich was visited by King Edward VII when a Royal Conferment ceremony was held in St Andrew's Hall. It was an occasion when His Majesty bestowed upon Dr Ernest E. Blyth and his successors the Honour and Title of Lord Mayor. The City of Norwich as the chief city of East Anglia had always enjoyed a close relationship with His Majesty. It was also an occasion when the city's trams found a new role. Apart from catering for the very heavy traffic, numerous cars were positioned at various vantage points and used as grandstands. Charges were made at 1/- on top and 6d inside.

Two years later, in 1911, the 10 trailer cars were withdrawn since they had not proved a success. Five of them (43–47) were motorised and they worked the route from Aylsham Road to Trowse. In 1914, just prior to the First World War, the tramway company obtained powers to construct a number of additional routes but the onset of hostilities meant they had to be abandoned. Not only were metals in short supply but coal was also short and manpower was reduced. As the war progressed services were curtailed and many late journeys were stopped.

Near the end of the war the War Department established an aerodrome and armaments factory to the north-east of the city just beyond Mousehold Heath. Since transport to the site for materials was necessary, the War Department asked the Norwich Electric Tramways Company if it could help. The company agreed to build a light railway to the factory but the necessary materials were at that time not available. The problem was solved when rails in King Street were lifted following the cutting back of the Aylsham Road to Trowse route to the Royal Hotel, which left Trowse isolated. A single track covering just over ½ mile was laid across the heath, using the King Street rails laid on wooden sleepers. At the factory several sidings radiated from a loop, beyond which a small steam locomotive was used.

Two freight motors, Government-owned, were built by the tramway company and used to haul flat cars, providing a link between the aerodrome and Thorpe railway station. At the station a single-track spur ran to the railway sidings where transhipment could take place. After the war the freight motors passed to the tramway company, which in 1923 used the units to build new cars (part of the rolling stock renewal programme of 1924/1925) but the track was not lifted until the 1930s when the tramway system closed.

After the war, using the 1914 powers, the service to Trowse was restored but now via Queen's Road and Bracondale. A branch from the route reached the Cricketers Arms at City Road. There was criticism over the infrequent service on these routes. It is said that a commercial traveller came out of a shop in Queen's Road anxious to reach the city as soon as possible.

A tram passes the market at Gentleman's Walk, c1919. The car is on the Unthank Road to Magdalen Road route. After the First World War further routes were constructed via Queen's Road to reach the Cricketers Arms at City Road and Trowse. (Pamlin Prints)

He noticed an elderly gentleman with a long white beard who was sitting on a public seat on St Catherine's Plain and asked if he had recently seen a tram bound for the city. The old gentleman replied with dry humour, 'I was a boy when the last tram passed here.'

The tramway company was proud of its freedom from major accidents. Often trams had run off their lines but without any serious injury to passengers. Yet two incidents were recorded. Around 1925 an Unthank Road tram ran off the rails and crashed into a wall near St Giles' Gate. At about the same time two Dereham Road trams collided head-on in thick fog near Nelson Street, one of the drivers being injured. Two other incidents involved men who insisted on standing on the open-top deck. Both were injured when they fell into the road, but not seriously.

In April 1925 the tram routes from the Aylsham Road terminus to the Royal Hotel and the branch via City station were closed and replaced by buses. On 24th March 1930 the route from Orford Place to City Road ceased operation. In the same year a special committee appointed by the City Council to consider passenger transport in Norwich recommended that the corporation should seek powers to provide a municipal bus service. It also considered that trams were 'a source of congestion in the streets of the city' and no extensions to the present system were desirable. Purchase of the tramways by the corporation, it claimed, was 'not a practical proposition on the basis laid down in the Tramways Act'.

In the original 1897 Norwich Electric Tramways Act, it was stipulated that the undertaking could be purchased 35 years after the date of the Act and thereafter at intervals of seven years. This meant that such powers could be exercised in 1932. The City Council was anxious to go ahead with the purchase although a number of members were against the idea. On 30th November 1932 Norwich Corporation promoted a Bill to authorise purchase of the tramway with a view to abandoning the system and substituting buses. A public meeting was held when the proposal was rejected by 314 votes to 275.

There were strong feelings in the city for and against purchase of the tramway company by the corporation and a Tramway Opposition Committee was formed. In the end the City Council organised a poll of citizens over the controversy and this was arranged for 10th January 1933. The opposition committee lost no time in informing residents about the costs that would be involved and how the ratepayers would be affected. Some 90,000 leaflets were distributed and sandwich-men carrying appropriate placards paraded the streets. The result of the poll showed 11,033 against the purchase and 7,775 for purchase. Despite all the publicity only 29 per cent turned out to vote.

Almost a year later, in December 1933, it was announced that the Eastern Counties Omnibus Company Limited had acquired a controlling interest in the tramway company. It therefore became inevitable that the omnibus company would announce its intention to abandon the trams in favour of buses, and it did this within a few weeks. Yet the trams were far from dead since during 1934 over 11 million passengers were carried compared with over 7 million by motor bus. The abandonment Bill finally received Royal Assent on 6th June 1935 after which time buses gradually took over the various routes.

The last tram (car no 10) ran on 10th December 1935 when it left Orford Place for Eaton and then returned to the tram sheds at Silver Road. It left just after 11 pm to the accompaniment of cheering crowds and the tram was packed with passengers. One of these was Mr Charles Watling, ex-Sheriff of Norwich who had also ridden on the city's first tram. According to the *Eastern Daily Press* of 11th December 1935, when the tram reached the Eaton terminus the passengers sang 'Auld Lang Syne' for the twelfth time. Its last journey to the depot was 'to a fantasia of cheers and bell-ringing' with a long trail of cycles and cars following behind. At the sheds the crowds joined

This building, at the junction of Silver Road and Sprowston Road, was the Norwich Electric Tramway Company's general office from 1926 until closure. The office was previously situated on Timber Hill. (Author)

76

hands round the car and sang 'Auld Lang Syne' for, it was claimed, the 36th time!

After closure tramcar bodies minus their trucks and glass were available for purchase at £5 each. Orford Place, once a tramway centre, is today a pedestrianised area. It was narrowed following rebuilding after bombing during the Second World War. The tramway company's offices, initially on Timber Hill, moved in 1926 to a building in Silver Road adjoining the tram depot. The tram depot has now gone, the site having become an estate of houses known as Bellingham Court.

8
Snow Halts A Tramway System

The Peterborough Electric Traction Company

Long Causeway, c1906. Car no 11 awaits return to the Lincoln Road depot. The city's trams operated on a 3ft 6in gauge track with current collection from overhead wires. (Lens of Sutton)

'Peterborough's electric trams are no more! Their death has been long and lingering, but nonetheless slow but sure, to the great relief of all concerned. They have retired creaking and groaning with age, a few at a time; the funeral has been drawn out, until at last the hardiest car of the bunch has got so tired of wandering to Walton, nosing to Newark and dashing down to Dogsthorpe that it has thought fit to go to the retired list.' So wrote a reporter of the *Peterborough Citizen* in its edition of 18th November 1930 following the closure of the city's tramway system three days previously.

Twenty-seven years earlier the mood had been quite different. When the first car left the Market Place at noon on Saturday, 24th January 1903, the crowds were so dense that many were left behind. The *Peterborough Citizen* reported that by 3 pm the car had carried 600 passengers – 200 an hour! Other cars soon followed equally packed with passengers. Yet the day was not without its humorous incidents. In the publication *Peterborough Tramways*, G.D. Austin writes that an elderly lady from the country was so lost in admiration of the trams that she let her purse drop to the ground instead of into her pocket. Fortunately for her it was found by Mrs Barlow, wife of the Dean of Peterborough, who handed it to the police who later returned it to the worried passenger.

Perhaps more bizarre was the consternation caused when a labourer on Market Hill saw a tramcar approaching Long Causeway from Westgate Corner and thought it was a Great Northern Railway train which had broken loose and such was his fear that he immediately had a fit. The incident caused quite an upset among the onlookers and it took seven or eight men to hold down the terrified man. That evening a minor incident had a happier ending. A domestic cat crossing Lincoln Road crouched with fear as a tram approached with its blaze of light – right in the cat's path. The driver humanely stopped the tram thinking he had run the cat over but on checking found the animal in the lifeguard at the front and all was well. Despite the saving of its life, the cat greatly resented all efforts to dislodge it.

Henry VIII gave Peterborough, on the river Nene, its cathedral status in 1541 and its town hall was built in 1671. Before the railways came, Peterborough was a compact market town clustered around its cathedral but when the Great Northern Railway sited locomotive sheds at New England in 1853, a ribbon development of houses soon linked the two areas. During the years 1879–80 efforts were made to

Car no 3 in Long Causeway looking towards Barrett's Corner, c1910. Peterborough's tramway system was a small one comprising in all 14 cars and a track-watering vehicle. All came from the Brush Electrical Engineering works at Loughborough. (Lens of Sutton)

build a horse tramway but none succeeded. This was despite the granting of a Provisional Order in 1880 under the 1870 Tramways Act to build a line from Crown Street (near the locomotive depot) to Peterborough North station (along Cowgate) with routes through the city centre via New Road and via Westgate.

Peterborough's electric tramway system was a comparatively small one with, at most, 14 cars and a track-watering car that could also be used as a snow-plough. Powers had been sought in 1899 by the British Electric Traction Company (BET) for lines to Walton, Dogsthorpe, Newark, Woodston and Stanground. A line to Stanground and a circular route through Woodston were refused because Narrow Bridge Street was, as its name implies, too narrow and also because of the difficulties in crossing the Great Eastern Railway line on the same level. Work to construct the remaining routes began on

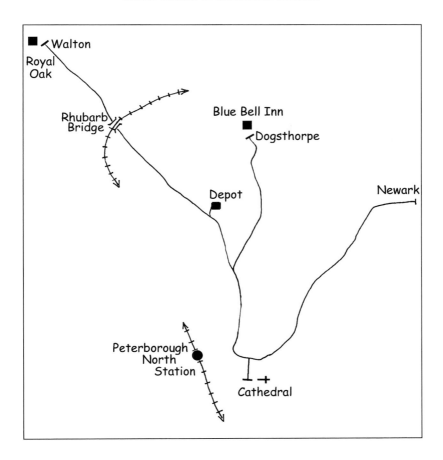

12th May 1902 but even this was not without its difficulties.

One instance, during October 1902, came about when the contractors were asked by the council to stop work for a week because of traffic congestion during Bridge Fair. The contractors refused so the council surveyor impounded the tar boilers and equipment, locking them up in the council depot yard. The contractors obtained further supplies and hired a number of hefty Irish labourers to stand guard over the work.

There were complaints too about the labourers and a councillor claimed the workers were rough and uncouth. 'It is shameful', he said, 'that young ladies of genteel upbringing cannot go out for a walk without having to avert their gaze and block up their ears.'

The 3 ft 6 in gauge overhead wire system opened on 24th January 1903 between Walton and Long Causeway with a route to Dogsthorpe following one week later. Newark was reached on 28th March 1903 giving a total route length of just over 5 miles. A depot and offices were built in Lincoln Road at a cost of £3,000. The depot consisted of five roads, which converged to a single line junction in Lincoln Road facing the city. The points were unusual since they were changed by railway-type point levers.

The cars, all open-topped and supplied by the Brush Electrical Engineering Co Ltd at Loughborough, were each equipped with two motors, both of 17 hp, sufficient for the town's level terrain. The first 12 cars seated 22 passengers inside and 26 on top on transverse reversible wooden garden-type seats. The original order had been for 14 cars but the last two went instead to the South Staffordshire Tramways to become nos 28 and 29. Cars 14 and 15 (no number 13!), acquired two years later, accommodated 28 on top. These were intended originally for Worcester but were diverted to Peterborough. The livery was lake brown and cream except for the Worcester cars, which remained the holly green and cream of the Worcester company until repainted.

In 1907 the turbine manufacturing company Peter Brotherhood came to Peterborough from London, which meant increased passengers on the Walton route. This led eventually to three extra trams being allocated to the early morning workmen's service. These were usually packed to capacity even to the point that overflow passengers had to hang onto the outside of the car. The Peter Brotherhood company was sited just north of the Midland & Great Northern Railway (M&GN) bridge across Lincoln Road. This acquired the name of Rhubarb Bridge when the line was built

Car no 11 at Long Causeway, c1906. Trams were proposed to the south side of Peterborough but lines were never built because of narrow streets and also because the Great Eastern Railway strongly objected to a crossing over their tracks. (Lens of Sutton)

Long Causeway from Cathedral Square. The last tram went over 70 years ago and today the area is pedestrianised. (Author)

in 1866 since the embankments had been built up from nearby farms and rhubarb roots continued to flourish in the soil for many years.

During the First World War women and temporary drivers were recruited, as in other systems, to take the place of those called to the front. Headlamps were masked as a precaution against Zeppelin raids. In the event of a raid, drivers were instructed to put out all lights and return to the depot immediately. Spares became difficult to obtain with manufacturers engaged on war work and services were curtailed, particularly on the Newark and Dogsthorpe routes. During 1916 Peterborough had not only the war to contend with but also weather of a violence hitherto unknown. A thunderstorm which started early in the morning on 28th March continued until 6 pm that evening when it was followed by a hurricane and a very heavy fall of snow. There was considerable damage with many telegraph poles blown down, some at Walton falling across the tramway's overhead wires halting services. The town was practically cut off and trams were disrupted for some considerable time.

During the General Strike in 1926 the trams stopped completely. A temporary bus service was organised, manned by volunteers, although the *Peterborough Citizen* was careful not to give names in its report but merely called them 'distinguished young citizens' and the conductresses 'dainty young misses of good family'. Yet the buses were not newcomers to the city's streets since the tramway company had been running bus services to areas not covered by trams since as early as 1913. In 1930 the city council was approached to obtain its views on abandoning the trams altogether. A sub-committee was established and it was provisionally agreed the trams should operate for the greater part of 1930 with abandonment commencing on Monday, 4th August of that year.

This arrangement began as agreed with double-decker buses operating various routes. Yet since official authority to abandon the trams had not yet been given, the company was

A Walton-bound car (no 9) in Westgate with Midgate beyond. During the tramway system's life, trams carried some 50 million passengers and covered between 6 and 7 million miles. (Lens of Sutton)

Westgate and Midgate, Peterborough, viewed in September 1990. There is virtually nothing left of the old tramway – the Lincoln Road depot now serves buses with the original tram shed partly rebuilt and the track removed. (Author)

obliged to continue its services to maintain statutory rights. This was carried out by running a single car over each route from 6 am to 7 pm, a vehicle that was quickly named by the local press as 'the ghost tram'. Eventually on Saturday, 15th November 1930 at 2.40 pm the 'ghost tram' began its last journey from the Market Place to the depot. The driver was motorman E.J. Jennings who had driven the first service car on 24th January 1903, and the conductress was Miss G. Coles. There were ten passengers.

Thus ended 27 years of faithful service with the trams having travelled between 6 and 7 million miles and having carried some 50 million passengers. Today there is very little to show that the trams existed. Several car bodies went to serve on farms and in 1975 one still existed in Crown Street, Peterborough, in use as a greenhouse. By the early 1970s all traces of tram standards had gone. The depot in Lincoln Road became a bus depot with the original tram building truncated and the track removed. A member of the staff at the depot proudly claimed he had a yard length of tram track at his home!

After closure of the tram services the *Peterborough Advertiser* announced in heavy type, 'The Trams have all gone to the Big Tram Depot in the Sky'. The *Peterborough Citizen* wrote less dramatically: 'Our famous trams are no more. They came, heralded by the whole populace. They went unhonoured and unsung.'

9
Trams Along
The Estuary

Southend-on-Sea Corporation Light Railways

Open top car no 8 at Southchurch village, c1903, at the junction of Southchurch Road and Southchurch Boulevard. The public house, centre picture, is the White Horse. (Lens of Sutton)

When Southend's trams began their first day of public operation, there were numerous problems. Many of the staff had received only a week of training and it was not surprising that at passing loops numerous trolley arms became detached from the overhead wires. There were also breakdowns and minor collisions. To make matters worse there were occasional failures in current supply from the power station.

The system was formally opened on 19th July 1901 by local dignitaries, with passenger services commencing immediately. Fortunately there were no serious accidents on the first day and, with the holiday season beginning, the difficulties proved more a novelty to the crowds than a problem. Many of those present were Londoners on holiday and it was the first time for most of them that they had seen an electric tram. Consequently traffic was heavy and every available car was in use. Even the lack of route indicators on the cars failed to dampen any spirits with the conductor having to shout out the destination at each stop.

In the early part of the 19th century Southend was a small village in the southern part of the parish of Prittlewell, referred to as the 'south end'. There had been attempts to rival Brighton as a 'watering place' but the lack of travel facilities had made this difficult. Approach along the river Thames was also a problem due to the large mud flats off the coast. It was for these reasons that Royal Assent was given in 1829 to the building of a pier. When extended in 1846 it was of necessity 1¼ miles long and in 1851 a single-track tramway was built along its length. (The story of Southend's pier is given in Chapter 10.) When the London, Tilbury & Southend Railway came in 1856, the area quickly developed as a resort with many trippers coming to the town.

By the time the Great Eastern Railway reached the area in 1889 on a line from Wickford, the population had grown to around 12,000. The following year the Borough of Southend came into being and in 1893 the town changed its name to Southend-on-Sea. The number of trippers, particularly from East London, continued to increase with the area becoming known to many as 'the Cockney's paradise'. It was soon evident that, in addition to the pier tramway, some form of transport was needed through the town.

First ideas for a tramway came in 1883–4 when a line was proposed from Southend via Rochford to the ferry to Burnham-on-Crouch. This did not materialise but when the corporation extended its seafront in 1897 numerous companies approached the borough for support for the construction of an electric tramway. Since the corporation was about to launch an electric lighting scheme, it was felt that local interests could best be served by promoting a tramway itself. Taking advantage of the Light Railways Act passed the year previously, the corporation applied for a Light Railway Order to build a town tramway system with an option to follow up with inter-urban extensions at a later date.

Accordingly, in July 1898 proposals were put forward for routes across the town from Leigh to Southchurch and from Prittlewell to the seafront. Further lines had been proposed through Westcliff but when the local residents heard of this, the idea was fiercely contested and was withdrawn. In addition a proposed route along Pier Hill and Marine Parade was dropped because of finance and the technical difficulties in coping with the steep road. Work went ahead in February 1900 on a 3 ft 6 in gauge tramway with an overhead wire current collection system.

At first a total track length of just over 6 miles was envisaged with much of it being built along country roads. A depot was provided not far from Victoria Circus in London Road. Construction included a route from the Middleton Hotel by Central station to Prittlewell and back to the Cricketers, a line from Southchurch to Eastwood and Leigh and another via Southchurch Road to the Minerva Hotel. Unfortunately work proceeded more slowly than expected due to delays in placing sub-contracts and because of the unexpected gravelly nature of the subsoil. When little progress had been made at the end of 1900, the corporation insisted that one section should be completed so that drivers could be trained. This the contractor refused to do, so the corporation warned that if the whole system was not completed by Easter 1901, then legal action would be taken.

Meantime 14 cars were ordered from the Brush Electrical Engineering Co Ltd. These included two single-deck cars each with 20 seats, ten open-top cars each with 38 seats and two open-top cars fitted with bogies each with 58 seats. Two each

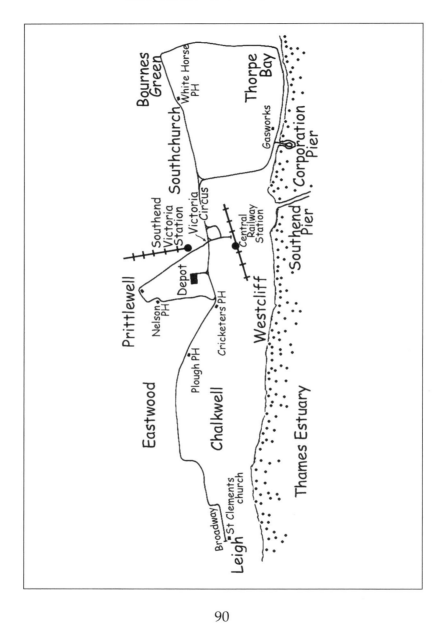

of these arrived in March with the intention that driver instruction could commence but when Easter came the contractor said that a further three months' work was necessary. As threatened, the corporation took legal action for non-fulfilment of contract and loss of earnings. Eventually, on 10th July 1901, the Board of Trade inspectors passed the lines (except for a short section not completed in Corporation Avenue) as satisfactory and public service began one week later.

The tramcars' basic colours were two contrasting shades of green and advertisements were carried on the 'decency boards' on the upper deck and the end screens. Longitudinal wooden seats were provided in the saloon, overlaid with carpet. On top, the seating was transverse with double one side and single the other. Lighting upstairs came from a lantern fitted to a pedestal at each end. There were initially no route indicator boards.

Open top cars at the London Road depot. Car no 36's destination board reads 'Cricket Ground' and the front panel advertises Dossett's Gold Medal Pastries. (Lens of Sutton)

In June 1901 a company known as the Railways & General Construction & Maintenance Co Ltd announced plans to build a 4 ft 8½ in gauge light railway line from Southend to Burnham-on-Crouch and on to Bradwell-on-Sea. Since the southern end was in the Borough of Southend's area, the corporation opposed the idea strongly. In November 1901 the company made a further attempt, but this time for a Light Railway Order from Southend to Colchester. Again the Borough of Southend stated its opposition yet at the same time declared an interest in itself constructing a section of the line, from Prittlewell to Rochford, but this was not to come about. At a hearing, the proposal to reach Colchester was turned down as impractical although some years of planning activity continued with the scheme last heard of in 1925.

Southend's trams proved popular although this was largely due to holidaymakers. The open-top single-truck cars were found to be inadequate for the summer traffic and in April 1902 three new bogie cars were supplied. These were the first

Cross-bench car no 41 on a 'circular tour' along Southchurch Boulevard. Sensible planning in the earlier times kept the tramcars away from the roads on preserved tracks. (Lens of Sutton)

A Leigh-on-Sea bound tramcar negotiates the reserved track along Southchurch Boulevard. (Lens of Sutton)

cars to carry any indicator boards, thus helping to avoid the frequent confusion caused at the High Street terminus. The two single-deck cars were used on the Prittlewell route where traffic was disappointingly light. Since it was only a short distance, intending passengers often chose to walk, finding this quicker.

Revenue remained disappointing partly because there were insufficient cars, so a further five were ordered for delivery in May 1904. These were built by Milnes and mounted on Brill trucks, each equipped with two 25 hp motors and capable of seating 64 passengers. Also during 1904 efforts were made to expand the system, Bryant Avenue on the Eastern Esplanade being reached by 1908. Agreement was given to proceed with lines to Bournes Green and Shoeburyness. The latter proposal did not go ahead and instead, after many years of delay and indecision, a short section of tramway was built in 1913–14 between Southchurch and Thorpe Bay, via Bournes Green, on reserved track thus providing a circular route. These

'Toast rack' trams at the depot off London Road. These were popular on the circular route from the Kursaal along the boulevards. (Lens of Sutton)

boulevard tracks to the east of the town became a showplace of colour from the thousands of shrubs and trees planted by the corporation. This tram route soon became the subject of many colourful postcards that were sent to friends extolling the pleasures of a day at Southend.

The fleet now comprised some 38 cars with the two original single-deck cars having been rebuilt in 1907–1908 as double-deck cars each seating 44 passengers. Others had been lengthened to accommodate extra passengers and a number were rebuilt with canopies. With the new 'boulevard' extension available, three single-deck cross-bench 'toast rack' trams were purchased. Holidaymakers were able to enjoy circular tours that imitated the good revenue earners of Blackpool and Southport. The tours started and finished on the front at the Kursaal with no intermediate stops, providing passengers with delightful views along the estuary before turning the corner at Thorpe Bay to the colour of the boulevards. A charge of 6d was made for adults and 3d for children.

When war came in 1914 services were considerably reduced as holidaymakers stayed at home. With the onset of the German Zeppelin raids in January 1915, all coastal towns had to take complete blackout precautions. As the Germans used the course of the Thames to reach London, Southend became particularly vulnerable. At first cars ran with no lights at all but later dim internal illumination was permitted. In addition, tram headlamps were coated with white paint to reduce their beam. Destination indicator boards remained unlit so as to confuse any possible enemy!

In February 1915 components arrived to equip three wagons so that coal, arriving by sea to the Corporation Pier coal jetty, could be delivered to the municipal power station. A circular tram track had been constructed on the pier, located off Southchurch Beach Road not far from the Kursaal. The wagons had a roofed driving cab at each end with a trolley

Tram tracks seen on Corporation Pier off Southchurch Beach Road in September 1990. Southend was one of the few systems that carried coal by tram wagons. From February 1915 coal arriving by sea was taken from the jetty to the municipal power station. (Author)

95

mast between two hoppers. These wagons remained in service until 1929 when supplies were taken from the national grid.

Meantime the trams remained busy despite the war. With many troops stationed at Shoeburyness Garrison, a service to Thorpe Bay was much in demand and it was considered unfortunate that earlier plans to extend the tramway to the town had not materialised. Using Thorpe Bay as a terminus gave problems. It became necessary to leave ropes permanently attached to the trolley poles of the open-top cars, being the only means by which they could be turned. On dark nights this often proved difficult, with the overhead wire almost invisible, a problem also experienced at the High Street terminus. The situation was hazardous too for unsuspecting passengers moving about on the upper deck who occasionally received a hefty clout when the trolley arm was pulled too low.

As the war progressed, the system suffered not only from lack of maintenance but also from shortage of skilled personnel. In 1916 women were recruited as conductresses and the three open cross-bench 'toast rack' cars were temporarily converted to more practical use as saloons by fixing panelling and windows to the sides. The benches were turned round to form longitudinal seating down each side. Despite the problems of the war, the system struggled on. In 1917 the section from the Nelson Hotel in Prittlewell to the Cricketers Hotel at Leigh was abandoned. In July 1918 trolley reversers were installed at the termini to ease trolley turning in the blackout – just months before the war was over!

During the early 1920s further cars were ordered and the three cross-bench cars were converted back to their original use. In September 1925 the town saw its first trolleybus, with another following the next month. Both vehicles were used to supplement the trams on the Prittlewell route. The track on this section had never been relaid and was in a very poor state, so early in 1926 temporary repairs were put in hand. On 3rd April all services stopped due to the General Strike and it was only thanks to the help of many retired employees that a service of sorts was restored on 19th May until the trouble was over. Meantime on 20th April Parliament agreed that the Prittlewell trams could be abandoned in favour of Garrett trolleybuses. Yet for a number of years the trolleybuses could not cope with all the traffic, so for a time trams and trolleybuses ran a combined service.

As the 1920s progressed it was found necessary to improve the comfort of the open-top trams now facing competition from other forms of transport. Once Ministry of Transport objections to the fitting of top-covers on narrow gauge tramcars exposed to the wind were overcome, older trams were converted and new cars ordered. But draughts in many top-covered cars caused a constant source of complaint and an experiment to fully vestibule a car proved successful, so more

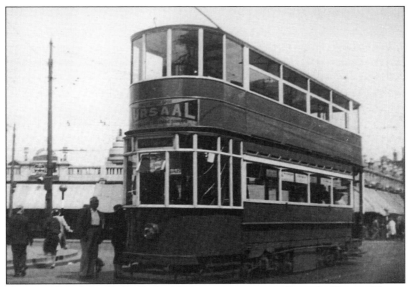

Car no 19, originally built in 1904 as open top, at Victoria Circus. Trams advertised the Kursaal, the extensive 'Luna Park' amusement area, as 'The One Bright Spot' in the town. (Lens of Sutton)

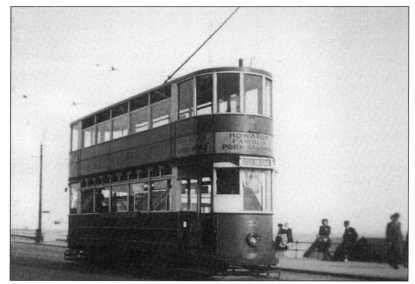

Car no 53 makes it way along the Thorpe Bay Esplanade seafront in the 1930s not far from Halfway House. During the summer months, there was a service of double-deckers between Thorpe Bay and Leigh along this section of the front. (Lens of Sutton)

were similarly converted. Further trolleybuses were ordered and the routes were extended. Despite this, much improvement was made to the central track layout, including the Warrior Square loop, and additional trams were ordered in 1934. To save costs and to replace older trams, these were bought secondhand, with four coming from Middlesborough and three from Accrington.

Economies were still necessary. In January 1934 the livery of the cars was changed to an all-over olive green and early the next year the local service to Thorpe Bay was cut back to the Kursaal, leaving the circular services to cope with requirements. The condition of many of the tracks caused anxiety and it was planned that the boulevard routes should close. In anticipation, a number of well-worn open-top cars were scrapped. The last tram ran on the boulevards on 6th July 1938, with motor buses taking over the next day. On other routes trolleybuses continued to take precedence.

When the Second World War came in 1939, the trams found a new lease of life as buses were commandeered. Petrol rationing caused many bus services to be withdrawn. No tram service could be terminated or tramcar scrapped without Government approval and certainly with Southend as a front-line town in the defence of Britain and London, no such permission could be easily obtained. It transpired that the winter of 1940 was a severe one and car no 19 (an open-top vehicle built in 1904) was taken off passenger services and fitted with snowploughs. In the saloon the seats were removed so that salt and sand could be carried. Occasionally services were cancelled during the Blitz but no vehicles were lost. The

Car no 58, built in 1924, seen at Victoria Circus in the 1930s. The tram route carried so many overhead wires at this point that it became known as 'cobweb corner'. (Lens of Sutton)

The numerous tramway artefacts preserved at Southend's Central Museum include this sign board showing the various destinations then available. The collection includes a number of badges and tokens plus a scholar's pass of 1918. (Author)

bad state of the track continued to give anxiety and it was blamed for the overturning of car no 57 on 19th December 1941 on the Southchurch route. Fortunately there were no casualties.

Finally, and somewhat inevitably, the Government gave approval on 8th April 1942 for the tram service to end. This stretch of coast was already existing under the tightest possible military security and most non-essential people had left the area. In addition the evacuation of children had long since been completed. To relieve itself of the burden of improving and maintaining the safety of the trams, the corporation had been able to show the dramatic reduction in passengers available to be carried. It was also able to demonstrate that the existing numbers of trolley and motor

100

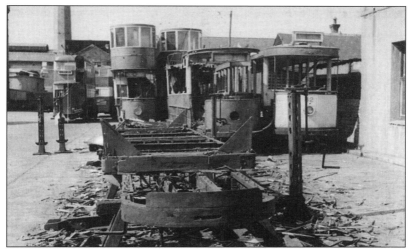

The sad sight of cars being demolished in the early 1940s when the system was abandoned. It was claimed that recovery of the tracks provided 900 tons of steel for the war effort. (Lens of Sutton)

buses could adequately handle all passenger requirements. With this in mind, the Government gave its approval to the complete closure of the system.

The last tram was driven in pouring rain by Councillor E.N. Selby, Chairman of the Transport Committee, under the watchful eye of Chief Inspector D.J. Grimwade who was a conductor when the system began 41 years previously. Speaking to council members and officials later, Councillor Selby talked of the many difficulties over the years and thanked those who had overcome them. He announced that during the system's life some 510 million passengers had been carried and of these not one had been fatally injured. This was surely a wonderful record and a tribute to the tramway men and women.

There is little left to see of the old system more than 60 years later. The tram depot has completely gone and the site

101

Southend Pier car no 8 which was sold to Volks Railway at Brighton, and was later returned to Southend Pier. It is currently on display at the pier's shore end. (John H. Meredith)

is occupied by a superstore. At the town's Central Museum a number of tram items have been preserved. Many driver and conductor badges together with tickets and tokens have been saved, also a scholar's pass dated 1918. Best of all, perhaps, is the length of tram blind giving various destinations in the town.

On closure, the *Southend-on-Sea and County Pictorial* commented: 'residents will miss for a time the noisy elongated vehicles which were such a familiar feature of our streets but their regret will be tempered by their appreciation of the superior speed and comfort of the trolley and motor buses.' The newspaper concluded: '900 tons of scrap metal have already been contributed to the war effort by removed rails and more will come – soon to join the garden railings in the smelting furnaces.'

10
Pier Tramways To The London Steamers

Southend Pier Tramway
Walton-on-the-Naze Pier Tramway
Felixstowe Pier Tramway

Southend Pier, 15th January 1949, during a period of single line working. Note that the 'winter' car has its sheeting down. (John H. Meredith)

Southend Pier Tramway

A wooden pier was constructed at Southend in 1829–35 and extended in 1846 to reach the deep water channel in the Thames Estuary. This was necessary to overcome the vast

103

expanse of mud that separated the water from the shore at low tide. By 1851 a narrow-gauge horse tramway had been built along the pier. Initially this was a cattle truck type car drawn by one horse but as its popularity increased so further cars were provided. These were coupled together and pulled by two horses in tandem.

In 1889–90 a new iron pier was built alongside the original structure and tenders were invited to provide an electric tramway. On Friday, 1st August 1890 the first vehicle, an open cross-bench car supplied by Cromptons of Chelmsford, had its inaugural run. The 3 ft 6 in gauge third-rail track was then ¾ mile long and the return journey took ten minutes. Regular running began on the following day and the public were delighted. Within three hours around 800 passengers were carried. By the next year a total distance of 1¼ miles was completed and a set of three cars was running.

Following the provision of more accommodation on the pier for steamboats from Tilbury, a prediction was made in 1909 in the *Southend and Westcliff Graphic* that the pier would need to be widened to allow for the laying of double track. The writer also ventured the suggestion that a tunnel might be built under the High Street so that passengers could travel directly to or from the railway station (now the Central station) but this did not materialise. By 1913 there were four seven-car trams, the longest ever to run on a British pier tramway.

In the mid-1920s some 25 steamers were calling daily during the summer and the number of passengers using the tramway was almost two million annually. As predicted, the pier was widened by 1929 and the track doubled with colour signalling added. During the Second World War the pier was taken over by the Royal Navy to become known as HMS *Leigh*. It became the control centre for shipping in the Thames for the duration, and in the event of invasion, there were plans that it should be blown up. Demolition charges were laid ready in place.

The tramway reopened to the public in 1945 and in 1949 four new seven-car trams were obtained. Built by A.C. Cars, their design was a cross between the modern Blackpool trams

The old and the new pass on Southend Pier on 11th June 1949. The press considered the new streamlined trains 'an unnecessary expense' claiming that trippers would not like them. They were proved wrong when up to 55,000 were carried during a single day. (John H. Meredith)

and a London tube train. Traffic reached an all-time high with more than 4,700,000 passengers carried in that year. For a few months the old and the new pier trams worked alongside each other but gradually the old stock was disposed of. Two of the cars, nos 8 and 9, were sold to Brighton Corporation where they were used on Volks Railway.

As motor transport increased in popularity so steamer traffic along the Thames reduced. Pier traffic declined and from 1970 only two trams were in use. When reconstruction of the pier began in 1974 only one track was used. On 29th July 1976 there was a disastrous fire when the entire pierhead facilities were destroyed. Two years later, on 2nd October 1978, because of council budget cuts and the poor condition of the track, the pier's famous tramway closed. In 1980 it seemed that the pier itself was at risk.

Yet all was not lost. Support came from the late Sir John Betjeman for a campaign to save the pier. Sir John said to a local reporter during a visit, 'Closing the pier would be like cutting off a limb.' A reprieve came in 1983. Funds were made available which, together with fire insurance proceeds, made possible the continuance of the pier and the provision of a new tramway.

Two new trams arrived, each with a locomotive fitted with a 55 hp Deutz diesel engine and five trailer cars. The speed limit was 10 mph and the cars were fitted with ballast to resist the occasional strong winds on the pier. It was a proud day in 1986 when HRH Princess Anne came to Southend to inaugurate the tramway and to formally name the trams after the late Sir William Heygate and, recognising his past interest in the pier, Sir John Betjeman.

These are the trams that regularly travel the pier today, with their popularity never ending. Yet no trip to the pier is complete without a visit to the Pier Museum. This was created in 1985 by the Southend Pier Museum Foundation (formerly

Southend Pier's diesel-operated tramway, July 1990. The first tramway to travel the pier was electrically operated, having its inaugural run over a century ago in August 1890. (Author)

Southend Pier's tramway track is today single and extends over the full mile and a quarter to the pierhead. For the vigorous it is possible to take a tram out and walk back! (Author)

Friends of Southend Pier Museum). Chairman Peggy Dowie had been a leading campaigner in the fight to save the pier. The Pier Museum opened on 8th July 1989 and it is today governed by a Trust. Open from May to October, here can be found a fascinating collection of pier memorabilia, including three carriages purchased in 1949, preserved from the tramway. The chassis and mechanism from the original 1890 tram can also be seen, on which has been mounted the body of a trailer car body found in a garden at Benfleet.

Walton-on-the-Naze Pier Tramway

The first tramway to operate along Walton-on-the-Naze's 2,600 ft long pier opened in August 1898. It was a single-line system of 3 ft 6 in gauge with no passing loops and electrically

107

operated from a centre third rail fed by a 50kW Parker generator. Rolling stock comprised a motor car and two cross-bench 'toast rack' trailers, usually with the three coupled together as one unit. All had been built by the Ashbury Carriage & Iron Co and mounted on Peckham trucks. The motor car's truck was fitted with two 15 hp Crompton motors.

During the 19th century Walton-on-the-Naze (once known as Walton-le-Soken) gained a reputation as a modest Victorian watering place. The resort's first pier, a wooden structure about 300 ft in length, opened in 1830. It was later extended to 800 ft. In May 1867 the Tendring Hundred Railway reached the town, causing the population to grow steadily. Walton-on-the-Naze actually preceded Clacton in popularity and the

Walton-on-the-Naze pier, 28th December 1948. The pier, destroyed by fire in May 1942, was rebuilt after the war and the narrow gauge contractor's line was adapted for passenger carrying. Note the baulks used by the earlier 'guided rail car' system. (John H. Meredith)

108

The motive power on Walton's pier from 1948 came from an 0-4-0 diesel locomotive built by Baguley of Burton-upon-Trent, works no 3024/39. It came originally from Wilson's Pleasure Railway at Allhallows, Kent. (John H. Meredith)

neighbouring resort did not get any trains until 1882 – at a time when its population was a mere 650.

The 1898 pier opened on the site of the original pier and was promoted by the Walton-on-the-Naze Pier and Hotel Ltd. During construction the company became known as the Coast Development Co Ltd, formed as a result of a merger between Belle Steamers Ltd and various other local interests. The tramway lasted until 1935 when it ceased operations. The track was removed and by the next year had been replaced by a rather unusual form of transport.

Visitors to the present-day Metro in Paris may well recall the system that runs on pneumatic-tyred wheels with separate horizontal guide wheels, and it was this principle that was adopted at Walton in 1936. A 20-seat cross-bench battery-operated vehicle, built by Electricars Ltd, ran in a 6 ft wide trough formed by narrow timber baulking fixed vertically to the deck. Horizontal wheels ran along the sides, 'steering' the six-wheeled car along the pier. It could be driven from either end, so the car did not need to be turned at the end of each journey.

On 30th May 1942 the car and much of the pier were destroyed by fire. When rebuilt, a 2 ft gauge contractor's line was laid and in 1948 this was adapted by Walton-on-the-Naze UDC to carry passengers. The system included three bogie 'toast rack' open coaches with a red and white livery, each seating 18. The coaches were hauled by an 0-4-0 diesel-engined locomotive built by Baguley of Burton-upon-Trent. The locomotive came originally from Wilson's Pleasure Railway at Allhallows in Kent.

In the early 1980s the rather ageing tramway closed for good and the only signs of it today are the odd pieces of timber baulking scattered about that once guided the electric cars of the 1930s.

Felixstowe Pier Tramway

First ideas for a tramway at Felixstowe came in 1873 when steam traction was authorised. It was proposed that a track should be built from Ipswich railway station to Felixstowe and then on to a pier still to be built. The plans covered 14.67 miles of standard gauge track plus a further 1.4 miles authorised from the pier to Fagborough Head. However, the main promoter developed plans for a port at Felixstowe, so in 1875 a railway was authorised from Westerfield. When this opened two years later, on 1st May 1877, the steam tramway was no longer needed and the idea was dropped. Meantime a pier had been built and a narrow gauge tramway provided a service between the beach and the pier. This was worked either by horses or a small steam engine hauling two coaches.

In 1903 there were plans at Felixstowe to open an electric tramway on another and more recently built pier. These were proposed by the Coast Development Co Ltd, which already operated a pier electric tramway at Walton-on-the-Naze as well as owning a fleet of paddle steamers serving the East Coast resorts. Construction of the tramway went ahead and this was duly opened in August 1905.

Like Walton, the gauge was 3 ft 6 ins and the track extended the ½ mile length of the new pier. Electricity was supplied from a centre rail, which was fed from the council's electricity works. Rolling stock comprised two motor cars and one trailer, with all three being of the toast rack design, each seating 36 passengers. The motor cars were fitted with Peckham trucks and they were powered by Thomas Parker motors. Since there was no passing loop, the three cars worked as one unit and the fare was 3d each way on a service provided only during the summer months.

Later in the year that the tramway opened, the Coast Development Co Ltd was succeeded by the Coast Development Corporation, which ten years later went into liquidation. When the company was finally wound up in 1922, both the pier and the tramway were acquired by East Coast Piers Ltd, which continued to provide the usual summer service. In 1926 one of the motor cars was given a new lease of life when it was fitted with a Westinghouse-powered truck taken from an old Ipswich tramcar purchased to provide various parts that were urgently required.

The tramcar was originally no 34 of the Ipswich fleet, which used the same gauge as the pier tramway. It was originally a double-deck open-topped car mounted on a Brush truck and built in 1904. It was not only the truck that proved useful. The saloon section of the tram was used as a waiting room at the head of the pier. The car fitted with the 'new' truck continued to serve until 1939 whereas the other vehicles had been scrapped by 1931.

When war broke out in September 1939 services were

After Felixstowe's pier tramway closure in 1939, one of the cars found its way to the amusement park for use as a shelter as seen here on 18th May 1952. (John H. Meredith)

suspended, never to be reopened. In 1940 the pier, like many others, was severed as a defence against a possible German invasion and during the years that followed the 'isolated' section became irrevocably damaged by the sea. By 1949 it had reached such a state of collapse that it was demolished. A new shorter pier was built, about one third of the length of the original one, but it was sadly without trams.

11
Trams Driven
By Steam

Wisbech & Upwell Tramway

Staff pose beside steam locomotives nos 136 and 135 on the Wisbech & Upwell Tramway. These locomotives were built in 1903. Some of these engines were later used on quayside lines at Yarmouth and Ipswich. (Lens of Sutton)

Constructed as a Great Eastern Railway (GER) venture, the tramway that eventually linked Wisbech with Upwell was mainly built to assist agriculture in the area. An early proposal for such a line came in 1873 from a man called Gillard who had obtained powers but due to financial problems the idea was abandoned. During 1878–80, the GER experimented with its Kitson steam tram engine no 230 from the Millwall

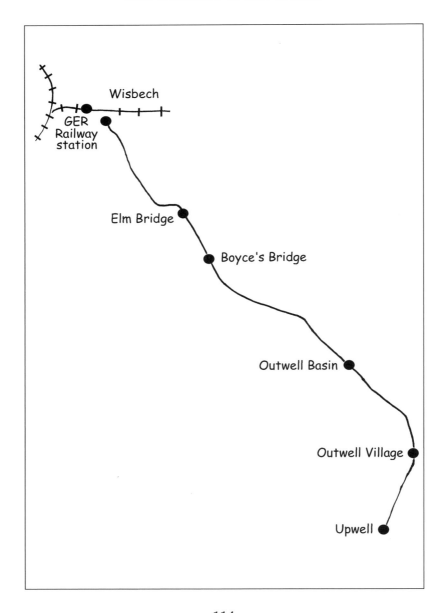

Extension Railway on London's Isle of Dogs. As a result in 1880 the GER resurrected the Upwell scheme by proposing a tramway to be worked by steam locomotives, but within the provisions of the Tramways Act of 1870 to cut costs.

An Act was agreed by Parliament on 24th July 1882 and construction began at once. On 20th August 1883 the tramway opened from Wisbech (GER station) to Outwell. The extension from Outwell to Upwell followed on 8th September 1884 giving an overall distance of almost six miles. For the first year of operation four-wheeled carriages only were used, with eight trams each way daily. Manufactured by Starbuck about 1870/1871, these were ex-horse trams which came from the Millwall Extension Railway. In 1884 bogie coaches were introduced. These had end platforms with ornamental railings and were provided with steps since the stations lacked platforms.

The Wisbech & Upwell Tramway, c1910. The 0-4-0 tram locomotives were fitted with cow catchers and warning bells and were enclosed in wooden casing giving more the appearance of a freight brake van. (Lens of Sutton)

A steam tram travels alongside the Wisbech Canal of 1794. The tramway closed to passengers on 2nd January 1928 but survived for freight until 23rd May 1966. (Lens of Sutton)

It is recorded that soon after opening some 3,000 passengers were being carried each week in addition to around 600 tons of goods. The standard-gauge track followed the bank of the former Wisbech Canal of 1794, much of it parallel to the A1101 roadway. In places the track was laid in the roadway, embedded in the surface so as not to obstruct road vehicles. Initially this was done with cinder ballast although in later years stones were used and covered with tar macadam.

The original tram locomotives were designed by Thomas Worsdell (GER Locomotive Superintendent 1881–1885) being 0-4-0 tanks. They had cow-catchers, warning bells and governors which shut off steam and applied brakes should 12 mph be exceeded. Enclosed in wooden casing, they had more the appearance of a railway freight brake van. Some of these survived grouping to become LNER class Y6. Between 1903 and 1921 a number of the locomotives were replaced by more powerful 0-6-0T fully enclosed locomotives (GER class

116

C53/LNER class J70) designed by Holden (GER Locomotive Superintendent 1885–1907).

Passenger services ceased in 1928 and six coaches were transferred to the Kelvedon & Tollesbury Light Railway and one of these was later used for the filming in 1953 of *The Titfield Thunderbolt* on a section of disused track near Camerton in Somerset. Tragically it was scrapped by British Rail. Goods working continued using specially equipped BR Drewry diesel locomotives but traffic continued to decrease. In 1961 the British Transport Commission announced that the line would close but such was the reaction from local fruit growers that the date was postponed.

The tramway survived a further five years but finally on 23rd May 1966 the end came. The last goods tram made its way along the track three days earlier, accompanied by a convoy of cars. Three enthusiasts even managed to get a ride aboard the three trucks and guards van. The *Eastern Daily Press* commented: 'No one could have described this as a memorable funeral for the 83-year-old line, the last link of its kind in the country. The occasion seemed to give the curious, rather than the genuinely sad, an excuse for an afternoon out. The Wisbech–Upwell tramway went out of operation quietly and even a little ignominiously.'

Happily for posterity, the body of one Wisbech & Upwell tramcar is still in existence. Car no 7, a bogie composite coach, was one of those transferred to the Kelvedon & Tollesbury Light Railway, but after this line closed in 1951 the car suffered the indignity of serving for over 20 years as an onion store on a farm near Ramsey. After 'rescue' in 1973, it was for a time with the Cambridge Museum of Technology but in July 1982 it was moved to the Rutland Railway Museum, Cottesmore, near Oakham in Rutland. The car returned to Wisbech on 20th August 1983 during celebrations to mark one hundred years since the line opened – its first return visit to Wisbech for well over 50 years!

The Midland & Great Northern Society currently own the car and it is in the process of being restored. From the North

Norfolk Railway it has been taken to the Settle & Carlisle Railway to undergo restoration in their Appleby Training Centre. The bodywork has been finished and in late 2003 approval was awaited from HM Railway Inspectorate for the design for new bogies. Once this work is complete it will be returned to the North Norfolk Railway to be completely restored to its original condition.

Conclusion

The Tramways Act, agreed by Parliament in 1870, initially brought about many road improvements at no cost to the local ratepayer but it proved a burden to the tramway companies. The Act originated from the days of the horse trams, when horses would wear out the road surface and tramway undertakings were committed to the cost of paving and repairing the roadway between the rails and 18 ins outside the track. This caused much aggravation in later years when the volume and weight of motor transport produced greater wear and tear on road surfaces than was ever envisaged when the tramways were built.

The decline of the tram has been as dramatic as its development. The first electric system to fail in East Anglia was at Ipswich, which was one of the first towns in the country to convert a route from tram to trolleybus operation. Three Railless/English Electric Company vehicles began services in September 1923 and within almost three years the trolleybuses (known locally as 'trackless trams') had taken over. A further three years later, in 1929, the small tramway system in Colchester gave way to motor bus services.

The first system to be abandoned in the 1930s was at Peterborough where, once again, motor buses took over. Yet despite the trams' 27 years of faithful service to the town's citizens, the local press unkindly commented, 'Their death has been long and lingering, but none the less slow but sure, to the great relief of all concerned.' Over the next five years, more towns bade farewell to the trams. First at Lowestoft, then at Great Yarmouth. When trams ended at Norwich on 10th

119

December 1935, it seemed the crowds that turned out to watch the closure were even greater than when services had begun 35 years earlier.

The tramway systems had suffered badly during the First World War with lack of repairs and severe shortages of materials. But at the same time, trams were more heavily used with many carrying workers engaged on war work. After the war the tram's popularity increased but the role of the motor vehicle in road transport was also increasing. In some parts of the country, the trolleybus was growing in importance.

Trams failed for a number of financial and political reasons. In addition to the problems brought about by the Tramways Act, municipalities generally underestimated the length of life of the vehicles and they had little experience of meeting the problem of obsolescence. Track repairs became a continuing financial problem. Tracks usually lasted about 15 to 20 years but often any allowance made for this had been spent on more essential work on the tramway. In the 1930s trams just went 'out of fashion', largely due to the publicity being given to the first really reliable and passenger-friendly buses. Another factor was the inability of management in some instances to provide through or extended tram services as towns rapidly grew in the 1920s and 1930s. As a unit of transport the tram proved uneconomic in the areas of low population. Overall in the relatively lowly populated towns of East Anglia, bus economics were clearly superior.

When the crowds attending the many tramway 'last nights' sang 'Will ye no come back again?' they little realised that around half a century later in many parts of the country such dreams could come true. Following closures, tramlines were torn up because the systems were considered outmoded, inefficient and an impediment to the growing volume of motor traffic. Yet today, as society has come to recognise more the nuisance of motor vehicles in the environment and their congestion of our towns and cities across the country, trams are seen as an alternative public transport system of the future.

There are currently no plans for trams or light rail

operations in East Anglia. Proposals do exist, however, where the technology requires the same legal powers to be sought as for a tramway or light rail line. One of these is at Cambridge where a current proposal enjoying local government backing is to use parts of the St Ives–Chesterton and old Bedford railway lines (near Trumpington) to form a track bed for a guided bus system. This will in part use ordinary public roads, providing a link between Huntingdon and Trumpington via central Cambridge streets where buses will not be on a guideway.

Despite press reports from time to time there are no plans at present to bring trams back to Norwich, although the introduction of a dedicated bus link between the railway station and the council-owned bus station is under consideration. This is part of a £9 million scheme to include new bus and rail station facilities.

As our towns become more and more congested, it is inevitable that alternative transport systems must come about. Failure to do so will surely lead to our town centres grinding to an eventual complete traffic standstill. In July 2004, however, the Government indicated that future schemes in Manchester, Leeds and south Hampshire would be rejected against claims of rising cost estimates. Sadly, one of the main disadvantages of our transport system today is that its future is in the hands of politicians.

How those early tramway engineers would have been appalled at the sight of our traffic situation today!

Opening and Final Closure Dates of Regular Passenger Tram Services

Location	Initial Opening Date	Final Closure Date
Horse Traction		
Great Yarmouth	1875	1905
Norwich	1879	1899
Ipswich	1880	1903
Cambridge	1880	1914
Steam Traction		
Wisbech & Upwell	1883	1928
Electric Traction		
Norwich	1900	1935
Southend-on-Sea	1901	1942
Great Yarmouth	1902	1933
Peterborough	1903	1930
Lowestoft	1903	1931
Ipswich	1903	1926
Colchester	1904	1929

Bibliography

In compiling *Lost Tramways of East Anglia* I have referred to numerous books, many now out of print, which include the following and which can be recommended for further reading:

Anderson, R.C. *The Tramways of East Anglia* (Light Rail Transit Association)

Anderson, R.C. and Gillham, J.C. *The Tramways of East Anglia* (Light Rail Transit Association)

Burrows, V.E. *The Tramways of Southend-on-Sea* (Advertisers Press Ltd)

Cobb, Stephen *Ipswich Buses – An Illustrated History* (Ipswich Buses Ltd)

Dowie, Peggy and Crowe, Ken *A Century of Iron – A History of Southend's Iron Pier* (Friends of Southend Pier Museum)

Klapper, Charles *The Golden Age of Tramways* (Routledge & Kegan Paul)

Markham, R. *Public Transport in Ipswich* (Ipswich Information Office)

Swingle, S.L. *Cambridge Street Tramways* (The Oakwood Press)

The Norwich Tramways 1900–1935 (Tramway and Omnibus Historical Society)

INDEX